IN A GLOUCESTERSHIRE GARDEN

Very little now remains of the exquisite garden of Bitton Vicarage near Bristol which Canon Ellacombe created during the last half of the nineteenth century and before the First World War. But in a series of articles which he wrote for the *Guardian* the Canon described how, season by season, step by step, he lovingly chose and planted the shrubs, flowers and herbs which drew visitors from near and far. These articles were collected into one volume and published as *In A Gloucestershire Garden*. It is reissued here for the first time in both hardcover and paperback.

The introduction to this edition is by Rosemary Verey, editor of *The Englishwoman's Garden* and herself the creator of one of the most beautiful gardens in England, Barnsley House in Gloucestershire.

The jacket illustration shows a detail of 'Cottage Garden in Summer' by W. F. Coleman, Christopher Wood Gallery, London.

Other books by Canon Ellacombe

The Plant Lore and Garden Craft of Shakespeare 1878

Shakespeare as an Angler 1883 (published privately)

In My Vicarage Garden and Elsewhere 1902

In a Gloucestershire Garden

CANON ELLACOMBE

Introduction by Rosemary Verey

CENTURY PUBLISHING COMPANY
LONDON

Introduction Copyright © Rosemary Verey 1982
E. Arnold 1895
All rights reserved

ISBN 0 7126 0027 2 (Case)
ISBN 0 7126 0028 8 (Paper)

First published in Great Britain by Edward Arnold 1895
This edition published in 1982 by
Century Publishing Co. Ltd,
76 Old Compton Street, London W1

Photoset in Ehrhardt by
Rowland Phototypesetting Ltd
Bury St Edmunds, Suffolk

Printed in Great Britain by
Richard Clay (The Chaucer Press) Ltd
Bungay, Suffolk

CONTENTS

INTRODUCTION

It was with immense pleasure that I learned that Canon Ella-combe's classic *In a Gloucestershire Garden* was to be republished. Each chapter is a gem in itself; originally written as articles for the *Guardian* during the years 1890–93, they are noteworthy for the sensitive way in which the Canon treats his garden throughout the year, for the attention he pays to each plant, to his favourite roses, to Spring flowers and Autumn berries alike.

He was a careful observer of nature and his writing entices one into the garden to see for oneself. 'If a fern is examined, the fronds of this year form the fine outside crown; but inside there is an inner crown which will be the fronds of next year.' We learn about his likes and dislikes. 'I see little beauty in carpet beds and pincushion borders; but the flowers which compose these beds and borders have each their own charm and beauty and we cannot do without them.' He may persuade us to take his advice: 'The grand old rose *Souvenir de Malmaison* is never so beautiful in Summer as in Autumn, so it is quite worth while to sacrifice the summer blooms, and let it bloom in Autumn only.' Botanical facts come through with tact and charm, when writing of the Christmas rose he explains that, 'the pure white flower is not as it seems to be, the corolla, but the sepals of the calyx. The true petals are curious little things shaped like trumpets, set round the ovaries, and soon falling off.' Surely an alluring way to discover botany.

When he was writing these articles the climate in many ways resembled our own recent weather patterns, with droughts and exceptional frosts. It is interesting to read of the effects these had on his garden and to see that every word of his advice has a background of gardening knowledge learnt from his personal experience.

For the beginner I can think of no better starting point than to read the first gardening lessons; not on how to sow seed or to plant but on how to observe and consider plants, how to enjoy and understand them. For knowledgeable gardeners there is a wealth of ideas to be picked up about best varieties, an abundance of new names to be discovered. Garden historians can learn which plants were fashionable in the 1890s and their history. This book brims over with anecdotes, knowledge and ideas written with enthusiasm and charm.

Canon Ellacombe is one of my gardening heroes; but it is impossible to appreciate all he has to offer, unless one puts him in his historical context, against his own personal background.

He was a great character, although his life could hardly be described as eventful in the ordinary sense of the word. Had he been a politician his career would probably now be history, but he chose a way of life which did not set him before the public eye, except in his own parish where he was loved as a father figure. To find out about him we must turn to his writings, to his books and articles, to his correspondence and the records of his exchange of plants with Kew – and to what others had to say about him.

Henry Ellacombe was born at the Vicarage, Bitton, near Bristol on the 18th February 1822. This was his home (except for one year spent as curate at Sudbury) for the whole of his long life, which easily spanned Queen Victoria's reign. It is a remarkable fact that he and his father before him looked after the parish of Bitton for a total of ninety-nine years. Henry succeeded his father in 1850 and remained vicar until his death in 1916 at the age of ninety-four. Because he outlived all his contemporaries, the anecdotes gathered in his biography, edited by A. W. Hill and published two years after his death, include few personal thoughts about his early life.

His education was typically Victorian: tutoring by his father, followed by Bath Grammar School and Oriel College, Oxford where he was strongly influenced by the Oxford Movement. He married in 1852 and had ten children, so for the ensuing years duties to his parish and to his growing family occupied most of his time; but when time allowed and the family grew up, his hobbies made him an extraordinarily good friend and correspondent and a much sought after host at Bitton. He was keenly interested in architecture, in archaeology, in church music and madrigals. He was a classical scholar and his library included old herbals, books

on horticulture and botany, works of the classical writers, and
much 17th and 18th century English literature. All this is apparent
in his writings, which are frequently enlivened by his apt use of
quotations.

His delightful sense of humour comes through in his correspondence. Usually brief and pithy postcards with a flash of wit
were his speciality. He was always exhorting his friends to visit
Bitton with typical sentences like: 'The garden is already full of
flowers but would be better for examination.' 'The garden is full
of interest, come and see it. If you could bring a bunch of Irish
Douglasii, it might add to your welcome.'

Miss Ellen Willmott was among his friends and she has left us a
delightful picture of a man she greatly admired. He was tall,
handsome and distinguished, with an intellectual countenance
and a courteous manner. He excelled as a host, for he loved doing
the honours of his garden, but if a parishoner called asking for
advice, he would go at once, no matter who he was entertaining.
Miss Willmott was a great collector of plants, so it was praise
indeed when she said that in order to know all he grew it was
essential to visit the garden every month of the year.

The first record of a consignment of plants from Bitton to Kew
is dated September 1869. On this occasion the Canon sent
sixty-five herbaceous plants and he received a parcel from Kew in
return. From then until his death the exchanges continued, until
several thousand plants had been sent out, as well as countless
packets of seed. In fact he sent his plants even further afield, to
botanic gardens throughout Europe.

Nothing pleased him more than to provide a plant in flower or
fruit which then figured in Curtis's Botanical Magazine; this he
did on nineteen occasions. His last contribution was *Zanthoxylum
planispinum*, a plant which particularly interested him because of
the way in which its leaves roll their margins under in Winter, so
minimising the leaf surface exposed to radiation and creating a
protection against great cold. The value of his services to horticulture is expressed in the dedication to him of volume 107 of the
Botanical Magazine by Sir Joseph Hooker in 1881—a much prized
honour. His gardening career continued for another thirty-five
years.

There are, however, two aspects of his life not associated with Bitton that were of much importance to him. A great grandmother left him a share in the New River Company (later to become the Metropolitan Water Board). He attended the monthly board meetings in London regularly and would then pay frequent visits to Kew as well as many of the gardens of his friends: Warley Place, Dean Hole, the famous rosarian's garden in Rochester, E. A. Bowles's garden. His friends near home included Marianne North at Alderley and Henry Elwes, famous for his arboretum at Colesbourne Park.

His other journeys from home were regular foreign trips to the continent. These entailed visits to gardens, searching for wild flowers in the Alps and Dolomites and for architectural delights. On 2nd March, 1903 he was met at Mentone station by Sir Thomas and Lady Hanbury and was taken to stay at La Mortala. He gives such a tantalising description of the garden, that one wants to hear more. Curiously, the Canon only kept a diary when travelling abroad.

However, the Canon's greatest happiness was undoubtedly in guiding interested visitors round his own garden and then sending them away with plenty of cuttings. Ashmore, who became his gardener in 1898, was soon as free-handed as his master; they both believed that exchange is the secret of gardening success, and that patience, liberality and catalogue are prerequisites of a good gardener.

After his death Ellen Willmott described his garden in this way; 'Although it was so old, the Canon's interest in new things gave it perennial youth.' You will enjoy his book; although it was written ninety years ago it has a flavour as modern as any present day volume.

ROSEMARY VEREY
1982

I am indebted to *Henry Nicholson Ellacombe A Memoir* edited by A. W. Hill in 1919.

PREFACE TO THE FIRST EDITION

This volume owes its existence to certain papers of mine which were published in the *Guardian* during the years 1890–1893. In republishing them I have omitted some, and slightly altered others, but only so far as seemed necessary in order to bring them into book-form.

At the time of their first appearance I received many kind communications and suggestions from readers of the *Guardian* and others. To all such I am glad to have this opportunity of returning my hearty thanks, as well as to the proprietors of the *Guardian* for kindly allowing the republication.

HENRY N. ELLACOMBE

BITTON VICARAGE,
GLOUCESTERSHIRE,
APRIL 1895

PART ONE

CHAPTER I

JANUARY

Introduction—The garden described—Cyclamens—Christmas Roses

EVERY garden has its own special and separate character, which arises partly from the tastes of the owner or his gardener, but still more from the situation, aspect, and soil of the garden. It is this that saves our gardens from monotony; if the conditions of every garden were the same, it is to be feared that the love of following the fashion of the day would make our gardens painfully alike. But this is prevented by the happy law that before success can be reached the nature of the garden must be studied, and the study soon leads to the conviction that we cannot take our neighbour's garden as the exact model for our own, but must be content to learn a little from one and a little from another, and then to adapt the lessons to our own garden in the way that our own experience (often very dearly bought) tells us is the best. And because of this special character in each separate garden it follows that each garden has something to teach, which cannot be taught so well elsewhere; and the happy result is that no one with a love for gardening who visits other gardens with his eyes open can ever go into a garden (especially if the owner of that garden is a true lover of flowers) without learning something. And it is this that makes the records of good gardens such pleasant reading; we cannot all go to Lancashire, Scotland, or the Thames Valley, but we can be thankful for the records of the gardens in those places as we read them in Mr. Bright's *Year in a Lancashire Garden*, or *The Chronicle of a Year, chiefly in a Garden* (also in Lancashire), in Mr. Milner's *Country Pleasures*, or in Miss Hope's *Gardens and Woodlands* (near Edinburgh), or 'E. V. B.'s' delightful *Days and Hours in a Garden* (in Middlesex).

With this conviction in my mind I think that a record of a garden far removed from Lancashire and Scotland, and even from Middlesex, with very different surroundings, and carried on under very different conditions, in south-west Gloucestershire, may have an interest.

I must first describe the garden. It is not a large garden—the whole extent, including a good proportion of lawn, being about an acre and a half, and in shape a parallelogram, or double square. It lies on the west side of the Cotswolds, which rise about half a mile away to the height of 750 feet; and about fifteen miles to the south are the Mendips. These two ranges of hills do much to shelter us from the winds, both from the cold north and easterly winds, and from the south-west winds, which in this part of England are sometimes very violent. I attach great importance to this kindly shelter from the great strength of the winds, for plants are like ourselves in many respects, and certainly in this, that they can bear a very great amount of frost if only the air is still, far better than they can bear a less cold if accompanied with a high wind. The garden then has this advantage of shelter; it has also the advantage of a good aspect, for though the undulations are very slight, the general slope faces the south; and it has the further advantage of a rich and deep alluvial soil, which, however, is so impregnated with lime and magnesia, that it is hopeless to attempt rhododendrons, azaleas, kalmias, and a host of other things; and it has the further disadvantage of being only about 70 feet above the sea-level, which makes an insuperable difficulty in the growth of the higher Alpines. On the whole, the garden is favourable for the cultivation of flowers, and especially for the cultivation of shrubs, except those which dislike the lime. With this introduction I go to the record for January.

> 'This is the state of man: to-day he puts forth
> The tender leaves of hopes; to-morrow blossoms,
> And bears his blushing honours thick upon him:
> The third day comes a frost, a killing frost;
> And, when he thinks, good easy man, full surely
> His greatness is a-ripening, nips his root,
> And then he falls.'—*K. Henry VIII.*, iii. 2.

This may well stand as the description of the gardener during the December and January of 1892–3. The first three weeks of December were so mild that many letters were written to the papers detailing the goodly collections of flowers that could be picked in almost all parts of the kingdom. Here I had an abundance of the bright flowers of *Cyclamen coum*; I picked several flowers of the sweet-scented *Chimonanthus*; the *Iris reticulata* was shooting so thickly through the ground that, knowing how rapidly the flowers are formed after the first appearance of the leaves, I thought it quite possible that I might gather some of the lovely blossoms even on New Year's Day; the snowdrops were pushing their white sharp points through the grass and in the beds in every direction; on many of the cottages there was a golden covering of *Jasminum nudiflorum*, and the China roses had many half-opened flowers. But Christmas Eve brought a change; then came 'a frost, a killing frost'—

'An envious, sneaping frost,
That bites the first-born infants of the spring,'—

and for three weeks a very low thermometer.

But, in spite of the cold, some flowers, though very few, bravely held their own; and though they looked sad enough while the frost lasted, yet as soon as the thaw came they brightened up again, and looked as happy as if the mild weather of the early part of December had met with no interruption. Two flowers especially distinguished themselves in this way, the cyclamen and the Christmas rose, and on both I must say something.

I am often surprised that the cyclamens are so little grown, for, with the exception of the Persian cyclamen, they are all quite hardy, they give no trouble, they may be let alone for years, and they increase rapidly by their seeds self-sown. The autumnal cyclamen (*C. hederæfolium*) produces its pink or white flowers before the leaves, and at a time of year when we have many other plants in flower, and so, though the flowers are very pretty and sweet-scented, they are not so much noticed; but they are followed by very beautiful leaves, which look like variegated ivy-leaves, and which keep their beauty all through the winter and spring. But for January we have the cyclamen of the south and east of Europe (*C. coum*), which produces abundances of flowers, not so large as the autumnal species, but of a rich red (sometimes white) colour, and so freely producing plants from self-sown seeds, that I am sure I am not exaggerating when I say that I have hundreds of plants, many of them growing far away from the parent plants. I suppose they like the soil here, and though they are mostly wood plants I grow them under a south wall, as I do most plants that flower early in the year, for I think such early visitors deserve all the help and shelter we can give them. I wonder that those who have woods do not try to naturalise the cyclamen, but I never heard of its being so used; yet that it could be naturalised is certain, from the fact that it has found its way into English and other floras. But it is quite a southern plant, and is not found wild north of Switzerland, and there the native species (*C. europæum*) is a summer bloomer, very pretty, but not equal to *C. coum*, and not so easily grown, yet it grows on some parts of the Alps up to 1500 feet, and I have it from the Rhone Glacier. I suppose the cyclamen is an old inhabitant of English gardens, for Gerard named some places in which it was to be found wild, but Gerard's localities of British plants are not to be trusted, and his editor, Johnson (who had no scruple in speaking disrespectfully of him), says it was never found wild in England. Turner, in 1548, could not go beyond, 'I heare saye that it groweth in the west countrye of Englande'; and Parkinson says (no doubt with an eye to Gerard), 'There groweth none in the places where some have reported them to grow.' Still the mere report that the plant was found wild shows that it was at that time a common plant.

I have a decided affection for this cyclamen—partly for its early appearance, even before the spring is with us; partly from old associations, dating from my earliest childhood; and partly from the botanical and literary interest of the plant, on which, even at the risk of being tedious by speaking too much of one plant, I must say something. The botanical interest is chiefly connected with the curious habit of the plant to form its seed-vessel in the usual way, and then for the seed-vessel to hang down, and by a succession of coils of its flower-stem to bring the seed-vessel close to the ground, and there to bury it. The cyclamen belongs to the primrose family, and not only is it unlike all the other members of the family in this peculiar habit, but, so far as I know, there is no other plant that does the same. Naturally all who have observed and written upon the plant have noticed this habit, and there is little doubt that the name of the plant was derived from this coiling habit, though some writers (*e.g.* Cowley and Miller) thought that the name came from its round roots and leaves; but the fact that Pliny gives the name also to the honeysuckle, which has the same habit of coiling its branches, is to me a sufficient proof that this was the origin of the name. What special benefit comes to the plant from this habit we cannot say: it is easy to say that by it the seeds are protected during the winter; but that helps very little. There are tens of thousands of plants whose seeds are shed on the ground, and have to fight the battle of life through the winter; and why this particular protection should be given to the cyclamen above other plants is a riddle as yet unanswered. Darwin studied it, and could only say that it was a successful effort of the plant to turn away from the sun, for the protection of the seed, but could go no further; so there we must leave it. But it is worth notice that the same coiling occurs generally in the Persian cyclamen, but in another part of the plant (besides the coiling of the flower-stem), for in that species it is a very common (if not universal) habit of the petals when beginning to fade to twist themselves into miniature corkscrews. And in the same connection it would be interesting to know whether this coiling takes place in the double cyclamens (presumably not seed-bearing). I have never seen the double cyclamen, and do not suppose the beauty of the flower would be increased by doubling; but our forefathers had it; it is described by Parkinson, and appears in some of the old Dutch and French engravings of spring flowers, and, I suppose, it was known to Rapin (1672), for so only can I interpret his lines:—

'Græca peregrinis venit cyclaminus ab oris,
Corcyræ geminam montes peperere frequentem.'

The literary interest of the cyclamen is connected with the name. There can be no doubt that it is the plant described by Theophrastus, and Dioscordes, and Pliny, and mentioned by Theocritus; and the curious thing is that the long Greek name κυκλάμινος has held its own through the Latin *Cyclaminus* into our common English cyclamen. In two of the oldest English Vocabularies cyclamen is translated 'slite', but the name is not given in the later Vocabularies, and seems never to have been a common English name. There is an old English name for it, the sowbread, but I can find no evidence that that was ever a name in common use; it was simply the translation of the continental *pain de porceau*, *Pan Porcina*, and with one exception I have never met with it in English literature except in the old gardening books. The one exception is in Calverley's translation of Theocritus, and if Dr. Lindley was correct in saying that it is the common food of the wild boars of Sicily, there is a decided fitness in Calverley's translation of the Fifth Idyll, *The Battle of the Bards*:—

'Go to the river and dig up a clump of sow-bread leaves.'

But I should think that the plant was never sufficiently common in England to get a common name, and Turner (*Names of Herbes*, 1548), says:—

'I have never hearde yet the Englishe name of it. Me thynke that it might well be called in Englishe rape violet, because it hath a root like a rape, and floores lyke a violet or sow-brede.'

Certainly sowbread could never have been an appropriate English name for the flower: its scarcity would have forbidden its use as food for pigs, and I once had a practical proof that English pigs care little for it. I had a night-raid on my garden from a family of hungry pigs, and in the morning it was easily seen that they had been grubbing in a bed that had a large number of cyclamens in it, but not a single root was touched by them. Of the cyclamen, with all its charms as one of our best spring flowers, I have now spoken *satis superque*.

I must speak more shortly of the great flower of December and January, the Christmas rose. This, like the cyclamen, has both a botanical and literary interest. It has now been certainly proved that our Christmas rose is not the hellebore of the Greek and Latin writers, which was supposed to cure madness; they spoke of two sorts, the black and the white, and the black was either the *Helleborus orientalis*, which comes from the mountains of Eastern Turkey, or *Helleborus cyclophyllus*, which is found on Mount Helicon and Mount Parnassus; while the white hellebore, which was far the strongest medicine, is certainly the *Veratrum album*, which grows in great abundance on Mount Œta. Our Christmas rose, *Helleborus niger*, comes from the Carpathian Mountains, where it is so abundant that it is said to grow in millions, and where during the three months of August, September, and October, the Austrian and Hungarian peasants dig them up by the thousand, when they 'yield a golden harvest to certain Austrian Jews who call themselves plant-collectors.' This is comparatively a modern trade, arising from the popularity of the flower during the last thirty years. Before that few gardens had more than two or three plants, though it has been grown as a garden plant certainly from the beginning of the sixteenth century. Prior to that I can find few records of it, but when we come to the great gardening books of the sixteenth and seventeenth centuries the beautiful winter flower gets its full meed of praise, and from that time it was never lost to English gardens; but I do not know of any writer, other than the writers of botanical books, who speaks of it, except Erasmus Darwin (and he, of course, may be ranked among the botanical writers), and what he says may be worth quoting, not only because I suppose very few now read *The Loves of the Plants*, but also for the curious note on the plant:—

> 'Bright as the silvery plume, or pearly shell,
> The snow-white rose or lily's virgin bell,
> The fair helleborus attractive shone,
> Warmed every sage and every shepherd won.'

And the note is this:

'The *Helleborus niger* has a large, beautiful, white flower adorned with a circle of tubular two-lipped nectaries. After impregnation the flower undergoes a remarkable change; the nectaries drop off, but the white coral remains and gradually becomes quite green, and degenerates into a calyx.'—*Loves of the Plants*, ii. 198–202.

Accurate observer as he was, it never seems to have occurred to him that the 'large, beautiful, white' portion always was the calyx, while the curious little trumpet-shaped green parts which he calls 'two-lipped nectaries' are really the petals of the corolla, which very soon fall off. I have met with one other poem on the Christmas rose, by C. Mackay, but it is scarcely worth quoting;

and about ten years ago there was in *Punch* (Dec. 30, 1882) a very spirited set of verses on the flower, too long to quote *in extenso*, but I shall quote part of the first verse as a specimen:—

> 'Know ye the flower that just now blows,
> In the middle of winter—the Christmas rose—
>
> Though it lack perfume to regale the nose,
> To the eyes right fair is the Christmas rose—
>   A fiddlestick's end for the frost and snows;
>   Sing hey, sing ho, for the Christmas rose.'

Of the Christmas rose proper there are several varieties, chiefly differing in the size of the flowers and their suitableness to different localities; and there are many species. We have two in England, both of which grow in the Gloucestershire woods, *H. fœtidus* and *H. viridis*, and both worth growing in the garden, especially *H. fœtidus*, for its handsome and lasting foliage. For the same good character I grow and admire *H. argutifolius* from Corsica, which looks more like a dwarf large-leaved holly than a Christmas rose. I also grow and am fond of the many hybrids raised about thirty years ago (chiefly at Berlin) between *H. guttatus* and *H. abschasicus*; for, though they lack the pure colour of our Christmas rose, they produce an abundance of really handsome flowers in the early spring, and their fine foliage continues in beauty all through the year. A curious thing in these hybrids is that, unlike the Christmas rose, which is one of the very best flowers for cutting and keeping in the house, their flowers very soon fade after cutting. There have been many devices tried and recommended for curing this bad habit, such as splitting the flower stems, or taking away the stems altogether, and letting the flowers almost rest on the water; but I have tried them all, and succeeded with none.

Closely allied to the hellebores, and so closely that it was formerly included among them, is the bright little winter aconite, now called *Eranthis hyemalis*; it has the same trumpet-shaped fugacious petals, and is one of the first flowers of the year. I noted the half-opened bud of the aconite this year, on January 22nd, and on the same day a half-opened snowdrop, but they were both beaten in the race by the very lovely *Iris histrioides*, which was fully open on January 19th, and is a gem of the first water. This, then, may take rank as the first flower of the year, by which I mean the first of which there was no appearance before the New Year; for the cyclamen and Christmas rose may be ranked among the flowers of December as well as of January.

And so the flowers are again coming to us in their appointed course. As yet there are but very few, but every day will unfold some new treasure; but few though they are, they are very lovely, and almost because they are so few they are very dear to us, and we may well be thankful for them.

CHAPTER II

FEBRUARY

Hybrid Hellebores—Crocus—Snowdrop—Snowflake—Early flowering
shrubs

THE month of February has a very doubtful character. 'In
February the sun enters Aquarius', is the record of the almanacks,
and so Spenser describes 'cold February' sitting

> 'In an old wagon, for he could not ride,
> Drawne of two fishes for the season fitting,
> Which through the flood before did softly glide,
> And swim away.'

It was 'February fill-ditch', and Don Pedro laughs at Benedick
for having 'such a February face, so full of frost and storm and
cloudiness.' But it is not always so; and when we do get a mild
February it is a most enjoyable month, especially to the gardener.

The flowers which I recorded last month are still in full beauty,
the cyclamen and the hellebores—not, however, the true
Christmas rose, which has passed away, but many of the other
species, and especially the fine hybrids, which this year are
showing quite splendid masses of flowers. I grow a great many;
the masses get larger every year, and some of them are very
curious; for the hybrid flowers have lost their hybridity, and have
gone back to not one, but both the parents; so that I have clumps
in which both parents are growing *from the same root*. I need not say
that this is a very curious feature in vegetable physiology, but there
are many other such instances on record.

If any one was asked to name the chief flowers of February, I
suppose he would name the crocus and snowdrop; I certainly
should with reference to my own garden, for I am glad to say that
both these beautiful families revel here. I have large clumps of
snowdrops in every direction, and almost an equal number of the
old yellow crocus, which I highly prize. It is not, however, quite
the earliest; this year the lead was taken by *C. stellaris*, a very bright

little flower, considered to be an old garden variety of the common yellow; but in most years *C. imperati* is the first, and it is certainly one of the prettiest. It comes from Naples and the mountains of Calabria, and is perfectly hardy, but here it increases very slowly. Both of these were in flower before the end of January; but the mild February has made the garden rich with all the species that flower in the spring. There are more autumnal than spring crocuses—I mean more species; but beautiful though they are in themselves, they never can have the same value as those which come to us when the garden generally is so bare. The so-called Scotch crocus (*C. biflorus*) is another very delicate one, which will stay in the same spot for years and go on increasing, and when the sun shines a mass of them is like a mass of silver. But of all crocuses I value most the old Dutch yellow crocus,—not to be reckoned among the oldest inhabitant of our gardens; but so long has it been in cultivation that its native country is not known, and it has lost the power of seeding. There are many varieties of it, but the one I like best is one in shape like a bottle-gourd, or old pilgrim's bottle, and so is called *C. lagenæflorus*. Its peculiar shape and deep golden colour make it very attractive.

'At their feet the crocus brake like fire', is Tennyson's account of the herbage on which the goddesses walked to meet Paris, and he is not the only one that has spoken warmly of the golden crocus. It is tempting to quote some of the descriptions of its many admirers, but I pass them all by, to speak of one book only, which once was warmly welcomed, but is now, perhaps, almost forgotten, but which always comes to my mind when the season of the crocus and the snowdrop returns. I mean Forbes Watson's *Flowers and Gardens*, a book published five-and-twenty years ago, and which came with a pathetic interest, for it was written on a deathbed of great suffering, and which appealed at once to all readers by its charming style and beautiful thoughts, and was doubly welcome to gardeners by the way in which he lovingly pulled to pieces, as it were, the few flowers of which he wrote, in order to find in them for his own great delight, and to point out to others, the hidden beauties which can only be found by those who love them as he did. I do not intend to quote all he said about the crocus or the snowdrop, for he has three chapters on them, but

any one who has read the book, and who is now rejoicing in the
spring beauties of his garden, will thank me for reminding him of
it. Few, perhaps, can see in the flowers all that Forbes Watson saw
in them; it is a remarkable instance of the way in which a
thoughtful man can read his own thoughts into almost anything,
and perhaps into flowers more than anything else, if he is a lover
of flowers. Tennyson, in the *Day Dream*, says this may happen to
any man:—

> 'Any man that walks the mead,
>   In bud, or blade, or bloom may find,
> According as his humours lead,
>   A meaning suited to his mind.'—

Bell-lovers have said the same thing. 'He that hears bells,' says
Burton in his *Anatomy*, 'will make them sound what he list; as the
soul thinketh so the bell clinketh.' I will dismiss the crocus with
two lines only from Forbes Watson—'The yellow crocus is a
perfect flower, leaving nothing that we could wish to add to or to
alter'—and will pass on to the snowdrop.

Of all February flowers I suppose the snowdrop is the most
popular. Its thorough hardiness, its patience under any ill-
treatment, its easy cultivation, and, above all, its pure beauty,
make it welcome to every garden, and there is no more valued
plant in the garden of the poor, and in children's gardens. I
suppose no flower brings so many associations and past re-
membrances with it; certainly it does to me, for it has always been
a favourite flower here.

I not only grow a great number of the common snowdrop, but I
grow most of the species, and would grow all if I could, but some
will not grow here. The Crimean snowdrop does very well here,
and I like it for its plaited foliage, and for the pleasant story which
tells what a delight it was to our soldiers when they saw it during
the first dreadful winter of the Crimean war. It was grown in
England before that, but by a very few, and I fancy that all that are
now grown date from the Crimean war. Clusius, who described it,
noticed that it was sweet-scented, but the scent is very faint. The
finest snowdrop with me is *G. imperati*, from Naples and Genoa,
and in some years it is the earliest, but I do not often see it in other

gardens; and I suppose it is particular about soil, for a florist nurseryman admired it here, and at once ordered three thousand from Germany, and in three years they had all died out. I have another which I admire for its deep green foliage, though the flower is small—the *G. latifolius* from the Caucasus.

Something must be said about the pretty name, or rather the pretty names, of the snowdrop. The common name is not the old name, and certainly, to nearly the end of the seventeenth century, it was described as the white bulbous violet. Such a cumbrous name might do when the plant was only a garden plant, and probably not a common one, but when it increased and multiplied so as to be found in every garden, and was becoming naturalised in many places, another name was wanted, and none more fitting could be found than the pretty name of snowdrop, which was creeping in in Gerard's time (he gives the name very doubtfully), but which only came into general use by very slow degrees. I suppose it was adopted from the common names of the flower in its native countries, such as France and Germany. Its German names may be translated as snowflake, February flower, naked maiden, snow-violet, and snowdrop; and its French names as the white bell, the bell of the snows, the bell of winter, and the snow-piercer. The pretty Latin name *Galanthus—i.e.* milk-flower—was invented by Linnæus to distinguish it from *Leucojum*, which he restricted to the snowflake. I think it would have been better if he had reversed the names, calling the snowflake *Galanthus* and the snowdrop *Leucojum*. For I have no doubt that the λευκόϊον of Theophrastus is our snowdrop; he describes it as bulbous and the first flower of the year, and sometimes even flowering in winter, and coming almost at the same time as, but generally a little before, the dog's-tooth violet, and always before the narcissus, the lily, and the bulbocodium, and much used for garlands. This applies better to the snowdrop than to any other flower, and the snowdrop is a Greek flower, while the snowflake is not. It is also mentioned in two epigrams in the *Anthologia Palatina*, and the lines are so pretty that they are well worth transcribing:—

ηδη λευκόϊω θάλλει σὲ φιλομβρος
νάρκισσος, θάλλει δ' οὐρεσιφοιτα κρινα.— v.144

πλέξω λευκόϊον, πλέξω δ' ἀπαλήν ἅμα μύρτοις
νάρκισσον, πλέξω και τὰ γελῶντα κρινα.
πλέξω και κρόκον ἡδύν· ἐπιπλέξω δ' ὑάκινθον
πορφυρέην, πλέξω και φιλέραστα ῥόδα.— v.147

For a charming account of the beauties of the snowdrop I will
again refer to Forbes Watson's book; it is very exhaustive, and
says much for the sweet attractiveness of the flower; but I think
this is shown by no writer (and many have sung its praises) so
touchingly as by Tennyson in two lines, in which he makes the
poor dying May Queen pray that she may be spared just a little
longer:—

> 'I only wish to live till the snowdrops come again,
> I long to see a flower so the day before I die.'

Very shortly I must speak of the spring snowflake. It is a most
graceful flower, closely allied to the snowdrop, and does well with
me, but, unlike the snowdrop, it increases very slowly. Its chief
difference from the snowdrop is that the three sepals and the
three petals are all the same length, thus giving the flower a
bell-shape, so that it more deserves the name of bell of the snow,
bell of the winter, etc., than the snowdrop. It is not a true British
native, though the summer snowflake, which really only differs in
size and time of flowering, is undoubtedly wild on the banks of the
Thames.

I must pass by the hepaticas, though they may take rank among
the earliest spring flowers. I would only advise that they should
never be disturbed—they dislike removal and division. All the
sorts are worth growing, and easily grown,—single and double
red, single and double blue (the double blue much resenting any
interference), and the single white. There is a double white on
record, but I never saw it, and have been told by a good botanist
that it is the autumnal form of the single red. This, if true, and my
informant was a very accurate man, is curious; but there are two
distinct forms of the single white, one with red and the other with
white anthers, and there is a large blue Hepatica from Greece,

H. angulosa, which in some gardens is very beautiful, but will not grow everywhere.

I might well leave the daffodils for the March record, for they are flowers of March rather than of February, but there is one, the earliest of all, which comes into flower in the beginning of February, and seldom lasts into March. This is the *Narcissus minimus*, a beautiful little plant with the small flowers almost prostrate, and undoubtedly only a variety of the common *pseudo-narcissus*, but sufficiently distinguished both by the size and time of flowering. It is a curious fact that these varieties succeed one another according to their size. First comes *minimus*, which is followed by *minor*, that by the typical form, and that by *major* and *maximus*. Whether there is any connection between size and earliness of flowering I cannot say. Yet it is certain that all the early spring flowers are of low growth; and this succession among the *narcissi* may be only a coincidence; but it is curious, and, I think, worth noting.

There are some good shrubs in flower in February, though none of them very conspicuous. The fine Nepal Berbery, or Mahonia, is perhaps the most conspicuous, and both for its flower and foliage it is well worth growing, but it is rather tender, and has a straggling habit of growth which cannot be kept in order by the knife; it dislikes pruning. The dwarf heath from the south of Europe (*Erica herbacea*) is in full flower during February, and is certainly conspicuous enough both to ourselves and to the bees; and if after flowering it is clipped with the shears, it makes a very cushion-like mass that is pretty all through the year. Among other shrubs in flower the *Daphne Mezereon* attracts from its delicious scent, but its stiff growth prevents its taking rank among pretty shrubs, yet many admire it much, as Cowper did, and described it as—

'Though leafless, well attired, and thick beset
With blushing wreaths, investing every spray.'

Three February shrubs may be classed together, the *Hamamelis*, the *Parrottia*, and the *Cornus mascula*. They are all examples of Forbes Watson's remark that most of the early shrubs produce their flowers without leaves. He gives reasons for this which I cannot fully understand. The *Hamamelis* and the *Parrottia* flowers are simply bundles of stamens, very pretty, but not very conspicuous, and both foreigners; but we have one British shrub with similar flowers, with which I will conclude my February record.

I always look out for the little female blossoms of the filbert, and always admire them. Every one knows the male catkins, which look so pretty when the nut-trees are bare of leaves, and some know the little crimson blossom which is now open ready to receive the pollen from the catkin. It is very small, but if examined with a moderate lens it will be seen to be a bunch of bright crimson pistils enclosed within some bracts. As soon as it is fertilised a very curious thing happens, of which I know no other instance. The little flower is placed upon last year's wood, and if it were an apple, or a peach, or any other fruit-tree, the perfect fruit would be there also. But the nut acts otherwise; it at once starts away from the old wood, and forms behind itself a thin branch, four or five inches long, at the end of which it ripens into a nut; and as it so travels it carries with it the bract in which the flower was formed, and which at last becomes the pretty cup in which the nut lies. It is this leafy cup that has given the name to the tree. The Romans called it *corylus*, inventing the name from the Greek κόρυς, a helmet or cap, for which I believe κόρυλος is not found as a true Greek word. The tree is a native British tree, and the old British name was *hæsel*, a name which it is not at all likely was taken from *corylus*, but it has the same meaning, for *hæsle* is a cap or hat, and *hæsel-nutu* is the hatted nut.

I wished to say something about the pleasure that a gardener can get by watching the different ways in which different plants come through the ground; but I must leave that to another chapter, and bring this long record to a close with the hazel. Few people are aware how our true British Flora gives us almost no flowers for January or February, and, I believe, none at all for January. Of course, I am speaking only of the normal time of flowering, for stray flowers, either premature or late, may often be found; and I exclude mosses and fungi, many of which flower in winter, some very conspicuously, as the scarlet pezizas. But the hazel and the spurge laurel, and the two poplars, are, I believe, the only truly wild British plants that flower before March, and this may give us some idea of the debt of gratitude we owe to the old gardeners, who have made our winter gardens bright with Christmas roses, cyclamens, crocuses, hepaticas, and snowdrops. Since their time many other winter flowers have been introduced, but very few have yet succeeded in getting a fair footing. Why some have succeeded with us, and others, which seemed as likely, have failed, is a large and very interesting subject.

CHAPTER III

MARCH

Celandine—Daffodils—Dog's-tooth violets—Anemones—Spring shrubs—
Strength of flowers in bursting through the soil—Uses of frost

'MARCH cometh in like a lion', and 'March winds and April showers bring forth May flowers.' But however cold and blustering March may be, it is not merely a nursery for flowers to come in May; it has abundance of flowers of its own, both in the fields and hedgerows and in the gardens. There are perhaps no more welcome flowers than the wild-flowers of March; in the hedgerows are primroses and violets, and everywhere is the bright coltsfoot and the lesser celandine, certainly one of the brightest flowers of the year, and 'so called bycause that it beginneth to spring and to floure at the comming of the swallowes' (Lyte). But for all its beauty and freshness, I cannot join in Wordsworth's well-known praises of it, for it is a sad weed in the garden, springing up everywhere and defying the neatest gardener.

There are many more welcome wild-flowers, but I must leave them for the garden flowers. First, of course, come the many daffodils, which ever since the day of Perdita we have been taught to look on as the chief flowers of March. With the exception of the rose and lily, I suppose no flower has had so much written on it, and such loving praises given to it, as the daffodil or narcissus. From Homer downwards many a poet has so praised it, and few English poets have passed it by. Gower, Chaucer, Spenser, Shakespeare, and Herrick are among the early writers; and among the later writers I need only mention Wordsworth and Jean Ingelow, and I need do no more than mention the names. During the last twenty years the daffodils have been raised (or degraded?) to the rank of fashionable flowers, and much has been published about them, and everything that has been written has been thoroughly searched for and abundantly quoted. I would only draw attention to one poem of great beauty, which is very little known, by Aubrey de Vere. It is called 'Ode to the Daffodil', and is entirely in praise of the wild daffodil, and so it reminds me that though I place the daffodil among our garden plants, it is really one of our native plants, and surely one of the most beautiful. There can be no doubt that the common wild daffodil, or Lent lily, is a genuine native; it is found throughout the whole of England, but is supposed not to be truly native in Scotland or Ireland, though found almost through the whole of Europe. The beautiful family is now considered to consist of forty-two distinct species, besides many varieties and hybrids, and its headquarters are in the south of Europe. A few, however, are found in Northern and Western Asia, one in Teneriffe, and a few in North Africa. I do not know whether any grow in Egypt, but on the wreaths found in the old Egyptian tombs there are specimens of *N. tazetta*, which have kept their freshness wonderfully for more than three thousand years. None of the family are found wild in America, but as garden plants they are highly prized there, and are imported in large quantities.

The crocuses have not only been very abundant in flowers, but two of the species, the common yellow and the pale lilac (*C. vernus*), have held their beauty much longer than usual. I cannot say why it should be so, but here the sparrows scarcely touch the crocuses, though I hear from many friends. especially in towns, that they cannot grow the yellow crocus on account of the sparrows. I have plenty of sparrows, but they do not attack the crocus; nor am I much troubled with mice, which in some gardens work woeful destruction among the crocus bulbs. Now and then I see signs of a mouse, but a good garden cat and a few traps soon get rid of the little plagues. Once, however, the mice, or rather the small field voles, entirely destroyed a number of young apple-trees, eating all the roots away, but not touching any part aboveground. For some time they refused all baits, but at last I tried the Brazil nuts, and that was irresistible, and I have never had a similar invasion of the little creatures.

Before the crocuses had passed away the dog's-tooth violets were in full flower, and I rank them among the very prettiest of our spring flowers. Yet they are by no means common, and I suppose that arises from their very slow increase, for my own plants, which have certainly been here over thirty years, scarcely increase at all.

Though fairly common in the south and east of Europe, it does not seem to have been introduced into English gardens before the beginning of the seventeenth century, and then was considered to be an orchid, though really of the lily family. Some of the family are found in America, with spotted leaves very similar to the European plants, but the flowers, instead of being reddish purple (hence Linnæus's name for them, *Erythronium*, from ἐρυθρός, red), or sometimes white, are all yellow, or yellowish white. The common name, dog's-tooth violets, they get from the sharp little roots, and it has been their name for a very long time; but the tooth form is not so clear in them as in another beautiful spring flower, the toothwort, or *Dentaria*, now classed with *Cardamine*. The plant is closely allied to our cuckoo flower, or ladies' smocks; and we have one wild one (*D. bulbifera*), which is rather pretty, but very inferior to the Continental forms, *D. digitata*, and *D. enneaphylla*, yet an interesting plant, from its habit of producing little bulbils in the axils of the leaves, which fall off and soon form new plants, just like the bulbils of some of the lilies, or of the bulbiferous ferns. But the purple and white species are really beautiful plants, very hardy and very easily grown, and great ornaments in the spring garden; yet sixty years ago Sweet expressed his astonishment that it was not more common, and it is still very seldom seen. The roots are very generally, though not always, curiously like a set of teeth, hence the name;—

'The root of it being white and smooth and shining, as teeth ought to be, it was fitly named *Dentaria*, *Dentillaria*, and *Alabastrides*, and as fitly *Coralloides*, the divers round small knobs set together, whereof the root is composed, resembling the knaggy eminences of the corale.'[1]

I can do little more than name a few of the good flowers that make our spring gardens so bright. The *Iris orchioides* has a brilliant yellow flower, and is a great acquisition, introduced about twenty years ago from Turkestan; the different fumitories (*Corydalis*) make very pretty clumps; and the two forms, purple and white, of *Sysyrinchium grandiflorum*, from Vancouver's Island and the Rocky Mountains, are most graceful plants, and

[1]Cole, 1657.

come very early. Then the anemones are beginning to show their many beauties; the first here was the rich blue *Anemone blanda* from Greece, followed very closely by our own wild yellow anemone (*A. ranunculoides*), and that by the grand anemones of Southern Europe, *A. fulgens* and others; and before the end of the month the pretty Pasque flowers (*A. pulsatilla*) will be in full flower, and the yellow *A. palmata*, from Hyères, curious from being the only anemone that has two flowers on a scape. I have named enough now to prove that March has a rich array of flowers of its own; but as I walk round the garden I note many more, of which I must only give the names—*Scillas*, blue, white, and red; *Chionodoxa*; *Arabis*, sheets of pure white; mandrakes; *Alyssum*; 'polyanthus of unnumbered dies'; *Aubrietia*; periwinkles; starch hyacinths, blue, white, and yellow; *Sanguinaria*, very curious, with its blood-like juice; *Milla* or *Triteleia*; saxifrages, especially the large-leaved *megaseas*; *Primula auricula*, the typical yellow from the Alps, and *P. marginata*; *Pulmonaria*; wall-flowers; *Dondia* or *Hacquetia*, and others. All of these are pretty, and some of them very interesting, but I pass them all by to say something of the shrubs of March.

March is rich in flowering shrubs, some of them ranking among the most beautiful of the year. The old favourite, *Pyrus*, or *Cydonia japonica*, is really a grand plant in every way, and for more than eighty years has been the chief spring ornament of English gardens; and, being quite hardy and easily grown, it is often seen covering the walls of cottages. Though its flowers are more abundant, and perhaps finer, and come earlier when trained against a wall, it will grow and flower anywhere; and there are many varieties, differing chiefly in the colour of the flowers; and it is curious that here I seldom get fruit on the typical red form, but I every year get abundance of fruit on the white one. As a shrub, the most desirable is Max Leichtlin's form of the *Pyrus Maulei*, which is a low bush so densely covered with brilliant scarlet flowers that in some places it would be hard to put a pin between them. This dense flowering is one peculiarity of the *Pyrus Maulei*, a plant which has almost a sad history. It was introduced from Japan about twenty years ago by Mr. Maule of Bristol, who was so struck with the abundance and beauty of the golden little quinces, that he gave up many acres to its cultivation; but the results were to him in every way disastrous, and even hastened his death. With the *Pyrus japonica* I associate another beautiful shrub, also from Japan, but very different in habit and colour. This is the *Forsythia suspensa*, a shrub which grows to the top of my house, and is now covered with long pendent branches, many more than a yard long, thickly set with bright yellow flowers. This, too, is very easy of cultivation, but is not often seen; yet it is very useful for cut flowers, for the long sprays can be cut while still in bud, and will come out well in water. The red-flowering currant (*Ribes sanguineum*) is another old favourite, now in full flower, though it has great beauty even before that, when the branches are studded with the bright red bracts within which the flowers are hid; of this, too, there are white and double varieties that make handsome spring shrubs. The almond-tree is in flower in several gardens, and is very pretty, and full of pleasant associations; but I do not grow it, because the flowers are short-lived, and then the tree has little beauty to recommend it; but I do grow and like the little dwarf almond from Russia, which, at the end of March, is a mass of pretty pink flowers. Last year my plant was covered with fruit; they were about the size of peas, and did not come to perfection, but they looked like little buttons of grey velvet, and were very suggestive of the 'pussies' of the willow. And this reminds me that among the flowering shrubs of March the willows, both wild and cultivated, are very conspicuous; the 'pussies', or 'palms', are beautiful objects, and I grow several of the dwarf species. I consider one, the *Salix lanata*, from the Scottish Highlands, one of the most beautiful silvery shrubs that I know. I must only name the peach, whose blossoms are now very lovely, for I want to mention two shrubs that are not so common. The *Rhododendron dauricum*, from West Asia, is perhaps only a geographical variety of the rhododendron of the Alps, but it is almost the earliest to flower, and the flowers, though small, are very bright, and the shrub will grow in soils in which other rhododendrons would perish. The *Azara microphylla*, from South America, is a shrub that is always admired, but seldom grown. It is a hardy evergreen, and the branchlets being all on the same plane, the branches are like the frond of a fern, and it bears a profusion of curious, very small, yellow flowers, which, however, grow under the leaves, and are so completely hidden that they might be entirely passed by; but they have a most delicate scent, very like vanilla, which brings them into notice. With the two Japanese honeysuckles, *L. Standishii*, and *L. fragrantissima*, with small flowers but a most delightful scent, and often flowering even in January, I may close the list of March flowers.

I have said that there was great pleasure in watching the ways in which different plants come through the ground, and February and March are the months in which that can best be seen. The more I study flowers, the more I feel how little I know about them, and especially how very little is known of a plant by its flower only. The young shoots of a plant when it first breaks the ground are often of wonderful beauty, and are in many cases so utterly unlike the same leaves when come to maturity, that to describe a plant by its mature leaves only is to tell less than half its story. And this is only one of the wonders of young plant life. People sow seeds, and watch for the coming of the plant, but few note that every separate plant has its particular method of coming out of darkness into light, and we may be quite certain that that particular method is the only one suitable to it. Darwin noticed that some flowers break through the ground as arches, the flower being formed underneath the ground, and then coming up curled almost like a fern. He instances the parasitic *Lathrea*, *Helleborus niger*, *Epimedium*, and *Ranunculus ficaria*; I have noticed the same thing in some of the fumitories, and probably it occurs in other plants. Why these should act so differently to all other plants is a mystery. But the greatest mystery of this bursting forth of the plants is that it is done when the growth is at its tenderest age; when the shoot is tender and brittle it has power to push through everything that binds it down. Instances are on record where funguses have lifted large paving-stones, and in my own garden I have an example almost as curious. Many years ago I filled up a flower-bed, and brought a gravel path through the midst of it. By accident a bunch of white crocuses was left in the ground, and now every year there is a bunch of these white crocuses coming up through the hard gravel path, apparently quite happy in their ungenial position. When I look on that bunch of crocuses I get an excellent

object-lesson in the enormous strength of even the smallest
plants. The leaves and flowers of the crocus are apparently so
weak that a fly settling on any of them can weigh it down; yet they
can force their way through a substance as hard as concrete. From
another habit of many plants I get another object-lesson, from
which I learn that plant-life knows no rest. Many plants come up
in the spring at a considerable distance from their position last
summer. Roses will send up suckers many feet away from the
parent plant; the pretty Chinese poppy, *eomecon*, will come up
almost anywhere in the bed except where it was first planted, and
this is more or less the case with almost all plants which in our
country dialect are called 'rastlers'.

If we carefully study the revival of plants in the spring, we are
often reminded that 'great are the uses of adversity', even to a
garden. An Italian professor, Signor Goiran, has recently given
his opinion that earthquakes are beneficial to agriculture, 'pro-
moting a more rapid germination of seeds, a quicker rate of
growth in the young plants, and a distincter greenness in all
vegetation.' Few gardeners would wish to have such a help in their
gardens; but I feel sure that they are helped by what at first
seemed almost as disastrous, for I am sure that for the abundant
flowers of one year we are often largely indebted to previous very
severe winters. We may have to regret the entire loss of many
good plants, and no doubt only the strong ones survive; but the
strong have by it gained more strength. The enforced rest which
is necessary after the shock of the severe winters may make them
produce few flowers the following year; but the rest was just what
the plants wanted to enable them to recover all they had lost, and
to gain much fresh strength; just as many an active man is brought
to a severe illness by overtaxing his strength, but the enforced rest
will often bring back strength that he was fast losing altogether; or
just as a fruit-tree which bears beyond its strength one year takes a
rest in the next year, and then fruits with renewed vigour the year
after. And this teaches us that the true gardener is never over-
much disquieted by bad seasons, whether they are seasons of
drought or of frost. The half-hearted gardener thinks that all is
lost when he has lost one season; but the wise man's caution has a
very wide meaning: 'He that observeth the wind shall not sow,

and he that regardeth the clouds shall not reap.' The fair-weather gardener, who will do nothing except when wind and weather and everything else are favourable, is never a master of his craft. Gardening, above all crafts, is a matter of faith, grounded, however (if on nothing better), on his experience that somehow or other seasons go on in their right course, and bring their right results. No doubt bad seasons are a trial of his faith; it is grievous to lose the fruits of much labour by a frosty winter or a droughty summer; but, after all, frost and drought are necessities for which, in all his calculations, he must leave an ample margin; but even in the extreme cases, when the margin is past, the gardener's occupation is not gone.

CHAPTER IV

APRIL

Banksia roses—Fritillaries—Crown Imperial—Pæonies—Magnolias—Weeds

When we can pick good roses in the open garden we may surely congratulate ourselves that we have left the winter behind us; and April often brings us good bunches of Banksia roses, white and yellow. If only for its early flowering this rose would be a favourite; but it has other claims. Its pretty and almost evergreen-foliage, and its climbing habit, make it one of the best shrubs for a wall, and in a very few years it will reach to the top of most houses; while its bunches of very small (almost the smallest of all roses) and very sweet flowers, pure white or yellow (not so sweet), are produced in abundance when the plant is properly pruned and trained; but all depends on that. The flowers are borne on the last year's wood, and so the long shoots which are produced in the summer must not be spurred in, as most gardeners are tempted to do, but nailed in carefully, while old and useless branches are as carefully removed. The plant has rather an interesting history. The date of its introduction is not known for certain, but it was first described (the double white form) in the *Botanical Magazine* for 1818, as Lady Banks' Rose; but all that could be told of it was that it was a native of China, and had been introduced in 1807 by William Kerr. The double yellow seems to have been introduced about ten years later; while the single yellow, the typical native plant of China and Japan, has only been recently introduced. The curious thing about these three plants is that the typical plant, the single yellow, is by far the tenderest; and that while the single and double yellow are almost scentless, the double white is one of the sweetest of roses, so that I once heard an old gardener, whose chief pride was in an old Banksia rose which he managed to perfection, declare that when in full flower he could smell it though more than a hundred yards away from it.

April is rich in flowers, and so Chaucer chose 'Aprille with his schowres swoote,' when

> 'Zephirus eke with his swete breeth
> Enspirud hath in every holte and heeth
> The tendre croppes'—

as the pleasantest month for the Canterbury pilgrims; the month in which 'longen folk to go on pilgrimage.' Spenser described it as

> 'Garnished with garlands goodly dight
> Of all the fairest flowers and freshest buds
> Which the earth brings forth.'

And though Shakespeare called it 'spongy April,' he also called it 'well-apparelled April', and 'proud-pied April', and it is indeed so rich in flowers that it is not easy to select one which demands more attention than others; but in my garden the Fritillaries are a chief ornament in April, and a great delight. I know that they are capricious, and in some gardens they will not grow at all, but here they are quite hardy, and being let alone they increase freely both by their roots and seeds. There are a very large number of species (more than fifty, besides varieties), and I believe they may all be considered hardy, at least in the south of England, and are all well worth growing; but I can only find space for two, which, though the most old-fashioned, are, as I think, the most beautiful. First, there is our own native fritillary; and its popularity is shown by its many English names—such as, death bell, dead man's bell, chequered daffodil, lily, or tulip, drooping tulip, guinea-hen flower, turkey-hen flower, snake's flower, snake's head, and many others. On these I need say nothing; but the Latin name— *Fritillaria meleagris*—deserves a short note. The flower was sent to Clusius, towards the end of the sixteenth century, by Noel Caperon, an apothecary of Orleans, who at the same time suggested that it should be called fritillaria, from *fritillus*, which he supposed to be a chessboard, instead of the dice-box often used with such a board. Clusius and others, who were better acquainted with Latin, pointed out the mistake, and some suggested *Caperonia*, and others (as Laurembergius) suggested *Gaviana*, from *gavia*, a sea-gull; but *Fritillaria* held its ground, not only as the scientific name, but also as the common name, though Parkinson and others tried to establish the pretty name of chequered daffodil, but in vain. The other name—*Meleagris*—it gets from its likeness to a guinea-hen, and this name it has had for more than three centuries. It is a plant that spreads from Norway through the whole of Central Europe to the Caucasus and Bosnia, and is now admitted into the English flora, but is a doubtful native. It is, however, found sparingly in many parts of England south of the Trent, and may be said to be abundant in the meadows bordering the Thames, from its rise to below Oxford, and in many meadows it is so abundant as fully to justify Matthew Arnold's description:—

> I know what white, what purple fritillaries
> The grassy harvest of the river-fields
> Above by Ensham, down by Sandford yields.'
> —*Thyrsis.*

In some meadows, especially near Cricklade, nearly all the flowers are white, and near Cirencester a curious variety has been found, in which the white flowers and the leaves and flower-stalks are so twisted as to have gained for the plant the name of *F. contorta*. As a garden-flower for April the fritillary is a most desirable plant; however much it spreads and increases it never is in the way: and the leaves and flower-stems die away so soon after the flowering is over that it may be allowed to remain undisturbed in any garden.

The other fritillary of which I must speak as one of the grandest of April flowers—I might almost say one of the grandest flowers of the year—is the great fritillary, the Crown Imperial. It is a native of Persia, Afghanistan, and Cashmere, and was introduced into England from Constantinople about the middle of the sixteenth century, and at once took its place as the 'Emperor of Flowers' (Chapman), as the plant which, 'for its stately beautifulnesse, deserveth the first place in our garden of delight' (Parkinson), and George Herbert called it 'a gallant flower, the Crown Imperial.' Perdita put it among her choicest garden flowers; Gerard described it at great length, and with all terms of admiration, and the beautiful French and Dutch books of the period gave excellent engravings of it. From the first, too, it took the name which still remains unto us, and which was at once adopted in all European nations; and the name was happily chosen, for it does not imply that the flower was the emperor of flowers, but it draws attention to a very wonderful arrangement of the flower and seed-vessels. It would be hard to find any plant whose flowers are more completely turned earthwards than the Crown Imperial, yet each flower contains a clear drop of sweet water at the base of the petals, which remains steadily in the flower in defiance of all the laws of gravitation. But no sooner is the flower fully-fertilised, and the large seed-pods formed, than, in spite of their great weight, they at once begin to rise, till at last they range themselves in perfect order on the top of the flower stem, forming what it requires little fancy to liken to a well-formed crown with sharp jewelled points. And not only in its name, but in another very remarkable way, the beautiful plant has remained stationary. Though it has been in the hands of the gardeners for more than three hundred years, they seem to have been unable to alter, or, as they would say, improve it in any way; so we, at the end of the nineteenth century, have the very same varieties, and no more, that our forefathers had in the sixteenth century. I will only add, that my experience with the Crown Imperial has taught me to leave it alone as much as possible, and never to remove or divide the bulbs.

I very much admire the pæonies, both the tree and herbaceous sorts, among the spring flowers, and I rank them among the flowers of April, though they are generally not in their full beauty till May. But in April there is a special beauty in the young foliage holding the unopened buds, and the foliage is so very different in the different species that a collection of them makes a very pleasant study. Many are in flower in April; the first with me is always *P. cretensis*, a dwarf species, with very pale rose, almost white flowers; and this is followed by the very handsome *P. Whitmanniana*, from the Caucasus. This pæony has been introduced more than fifty years, but is still very scarce, though its large yellow flowers are very handsome, and give it the appearance of a gigantic *trollius*. When the flowers of the pæonies are past, their beauty is by no means over, for their foliage and curious seed-vessels are attractive objects in the garden for many months. I leave the dicentras, though I think *D. spectabilis* the finest hardy herbaceous plant that has been introduced during the last fifty years; the pansies, anemones, candytufts, and a host of other things which make the garden bright in April, that I may say something of the shrubs of April.

I cannot understand why so very few people grow the spring-flowering magnolias. Many grow the large *M. grandiflora*; but coming from the Southern United States, it is doubtfully hardy, and I have twice had it quite killed by frost, though the stem of the tree was 6 in. through; nor have I found it an easy tree to manage. But the Chinese and Japanese species are perfectly hardy, very easy to manage, and in spring giving an abundance of most handsome flowers. The species which I cultivate, and which have been in wonderful beauty during the month, are *M. Lennei*, with large flowers, of a rich, rosy red, and each petal looking like a fine shell, *M. obovata*, *M. purpurea*, and *M. stellata*. This last I think the best of all; it forms a low shrub, which is covered with small flowers of quite a dazzling white. The drawback to these deciduous early magnolias is that their flowers are apt to be caught by the spring frosts, but the same objection does not apply to the Japanese orange, *Citrus trifoliata*, which I have known covered with its white blossoms at the time of frost, but not a flower was injured. This is a curiously neglected shrub, for it has been introduced many years, and has very pretty foliage, and sometimes produces little oranges, which, however, are of no value. Other good flowering shrubs for April are the *Malus floribunda*, quite magnificent in bud; the Exochordas, very pretty in bud; several of the Genistas, especially *G. præcox*, and the double-flowering gorse; and even the shrubs which flower later are very attractive in April from their young foliage.

I am sorry to say that the April record of the garden would be very incomplete without some mention of the weeds; for it is in April they first show themselves, and some of them only in April. In new gardens it is possible, and not very difficult, to keep the weeds under; but in old gardens it is almost impossible. It is an old and very true gardening proverb, that one year's seed is many years' weed; or as Hamlet laments, 'An unweeded garden grows to seed,' and so 'things rank and gross in nature possess it merely.' In the history of an old garden there must have often been a one year's seed; and there must be in it from time to time many an unweeded corner. But I have almost an affection for weeds, a decided affection for some of them, and I have not much sympathy with those who say that a garden is not worth looking at unless it is as clean as a newly-swept floor; it is a counsel of perfection, which I have no great wish to reach. A weed is but a good plant in the wrong place; I say a *good* plant advisedly, having a full faith that where nature plants it, it fills a right place. Daisies are not perhaps in their right place in lawns, but I should be sorry to see my lawn quite free from them, and so I am sure would the children. Buttercups have a shining beauty of petal that is not surpassed by any flower, and I do not think that Jean Ingelow's comparison of a field of buttercups to the Field of the Cloth of Gold, to the great advantage of the buttercups, is much exaggerated; but they must be kept out of the garden. The weeds that chiefly trouble me in April are the two veronicas, *V. agrestis* and *V. Buxbaumi*; either of them might lay claim to the title of 'the little speedwell's darling blue,' and they are so short-lived that they do little real harm; still, they give a good deal of trouble. But some weeds are so beautiful that I should certainly grow them in the garden, if only they could be kept in place, and if they were not already too abundant. I should be sorry to banish from my walls the creeping toad-flax and the yellow fumitory, and as long as they keep to the walls they do no harm. But there are two plants that are sad weeds, but which, if lost, would be sorely missed. The dandelion is one—

'The flower
That blows a globe of after arrowlets.'

Surely no other flower can surpass it for beauty of foliage, beauty of shape, and rich beauty of colouring. The second weed that I often wish to transplant into my garden, but dare not, is the goosegrass, or silver weed, *Potentilla anserina*. Its beautiful leaves have a silver sheen that make it very attractive; but it is better kept outside the garden, and it grows everywhere. It is found in the Arctic regions and it is found in New Zealand, and so has as wide a range as almost any known plant, except, perhaps, the little fern *Cystopteris fragilis*, which not only grows as far north as lat. 76 deg., and as far south as New Zealand, but was also found by Whymper in the Equatorial Andes.

But it is not only for their beauty that I have an affection for some of the weeds, but, speaking as a gardener, I am sure that they are often very useful. We may see how in a hedgerow the most delicate plants nestle themselves close to and under those of the coarsest growth, and seem all the better for it; and I have seen many instances in which delicate seeds and young cuttings have been saved when protected by weeds, when those not so protected have perished. One of the most interesting gardens and the most untidy I ever saw was Professor Syme's in Fifeshire. It was a mass of weeds, and rampant weeds; but among the weeds, and apparently rejoicing in them, was a collection of some of the rarest plants, growing in greater luxuriance than I had ever seen elsewhere. The weeds keep the earth moist, and prevent the radiation of heat, and how much they do so most of us can see by observing the plantains on our lawns. I am not fond of plantains on lawns, and get rid of them; but some will remain, and on them I have often noticed that in a slight hoar-frost no hoar-frost is formed on the plantains; the broad leaves lying flat on the ground keep in the earth-heat. I am tempted to say more about weeds and their uses, but instead of doing so I will refer—and those who do not know the book will thank me for doing so—to one of Burroughs' charming little books, *Pepacton*, where there is a long chapter on the use and beauty of weeds. I will, however, quote another American writer, Hawthorne, who is quite enthusiastic in his praise of weeds. 'There is,' he says, 'a sort of sacredness about them. Perhaps if we could penetrate Nature's secrets we should find that what we call weeds are more essential to the well-being of the world than the most precious fruit or grain.' This is perhaps somewhat exaggerated, but there is a good truth in it.

CHAPTER V

MAY

Tulips—Genistas—Effects of drought

THE garden record for May ought to be a record of abundance of flowers and rich greenery, both in field and garden. But the May of 1893 will long be remembered as a May in which the garden was burnt up, and everything was thrown out of its proper season. There were flowers in abundance; but the flowers of May owed nothing to the April showers, for the long drought was accompanied with brilliant sunshine, and for the most part of the time with dry easterly and north-easterly winds, making the earth, even in the most favoured soils, hard and parched, and with little or no refreshment from dews, 'the heaven over our head being as brass, and the earth beneath us as iron.' The result of this was that the gardens, and indeed the whole country, presented an appearance such as few of us could remember, and produced many curious sights which might rightly be called abnormal.

Among these curious abnormal sights, I should reckon the hawthorn, of which it is generally very difficult to pick a single blossom on May-day, but which in that year was in full flower at the same time as the blackthorn, on the 13th of April, and was even in flower before the first swallow was seen. The swallows were very late that year. I did not see the first in my garden till the 23rd of April, only one day before the cuckoo was heard for the first time; and on the same day appeared the pretty little redstart, which I always welcome as one of the truest harbingers of summer, almost as much so as the corncrake, which I both heard and saw on April 25.

In the garden the chief effect was that the flowers were forced into premature blooming; we had in May the flowers of June. There was a wonderful abundance of flowers everywhere, but they were stunted, and starved, and dwarfed, and so were robbed of half their beauty. Thus the lily of the valley which delights in moisture, produced flowers which were like silver shot, and were sadly deficient in scent; and the beautiful guelder rose produced its lovely balls of flowers about one-half the usual size. The late daffodils came with short stalks and small flowers, and soon passed away; while many plants, especially those with shallow roots, or which had not been long planted, gradually flagged and in many cases perished.

Still there was an abundance of flowers, and among the flowers of the end of April and the early part of May none are so conspicuous as the tulips. I am not very fond of the florist's tulips; in some cases their colours are most brilliant, but always coarse and flaring, and their growth is very stiff, and to me they give little pleasure. Indeed, I think a bed consisting of tulips only is an ugly object; I should say that such a bed is the ugliest of all such one-flowered beds, except a bed of double zinnias; but in so saying I suppose I am in a minority, and perhaps a very small minority. For more than three hundred years tulips have had a wonderful fascination for all florist gardeners, and for many who are more than florists, and I suppose their popularity is still almost as great as ever. The bulb catalogues, both English and foreign, contain every year long lists of tulips. Many of them are very high-priced, though, of course, very cheap if compared with the prices which are reported to have been given for tulips during the 'tulipo-mania' of the seventeenth century. In the whole history of plants there is probably no more curious or sadder chapter than this of the tulipo-mania, which, though still often quoted as an instance of the extravagance of florists in their favourite flowers, is known to have been simply a gigantic swindle, in which the plants had really very little part—a Stock Exchange gambling, which it required the high hand of the law to stop. But it was not stopped before it had produced quite a literature of its own; and a long list of books on the subject will be found in Beckman's *History of Inventions*, who gives also an excellent account of the great swindle.

The tulips of the florist are all varieties of the Eastern *T. Gesneriana*, a plant which varies from seed and roots almost more than any plant known, so that the same plant cannot be depended on to produce the same flowers for more than two or three years.

But besides the florist's tulip there are nearly a hundred true species coming from the south and east of Europe, thence through Southern Asia to India, China, and Japan; but none are found in America and Australia. Of these, many are very beautiful flowers, and, unlike *the* great florist's tulip, are low and small. They mostly come from Central Asia, and many of them are of quite recent introduction; and among them I should especially recommend *Kolpakowskyana*, *Ostrowskyana*, *pulchella*, *saxatilis*, *australis* (called by nurserymen *Persica*), and *undulatæfolia*. I also much admire *T. retroflexa*, a most graceful flower with pale yellow recurved petals, which was a great favourite with the late Mrs. Ewing (Aunt Judy), and I think there are none more beautiful than the two European species, *T. Clusiana* from Mentone, and *T. sylvestris*. In my own garden I have never seen a flower of *T. Clusiana*, though it sends up leaves every year, but *T. sylvestris* is abundant in flower and very beautiful. It is the only tulip that can be called Northern, and botanists doubt its being a true native of Britain; but I have seen it in abundance on a barren hillside near Bath, far from houses, and where it seems most certainly wild, and it is almost the only plant that grows well there, except the Bath asparagus, *Ornithogalum Pyrenaicum*, which is equally abundant.

I must say something more about the tulip, for it has both a literary and botanic interest. Besides the literature on the 'tulipomania', which I have already mentioned, the writers of the seventeenth and eighteenth centuries seem to have thought that no words were sufficient to express their admiration of the tulip. Of course such writers are for the most part writers on flowers; for, in spite of the popularity of the flower, it does not seem to have found any such place in general literature as the lily and the rose. Herrick indeed was bold enough to compare his mistress to a tulip, but it was only to point the moral that life and beauty soon pass away; and I know of no other author who has made the tulip his subject except Steele, who, in a charming paper in the *Tatler* (No. 228), has a good-humoured laugh against the absurd names given to tulips, and congratulated himself that he 'had never fallen into any of these fantastical tastes,' but, 'looking upon the whole country in spring-time as a spacious garden,' could thank 'the

bounty of Providence, which has made the most pleasing and
most beautiful objects the most ordinary and most common.' But
with the gardening writers the praises of the tulip are absurdly
fulsome and extravagant. Each writer tries to outdo the others in
his superlatives, and I have no room for their praises. One
specimen will suffice, and I choose it because the writer, Francis
Pomey, a Jesuit of the early part of the seventeenth century, is
little known, and I quote from Hoffmann:—

'Tulipa, in regno florum, coronam sibi iure vindicat. Huic uni concessit
natura, ut quidquid venustatis et gratiæ aliis tributum dispersumque est, ipsa in
se colligat.'

There is much more to the same effect, but that is enough, for I
want to say something about a very curious point in the botanical
structure of the tulip. The flower of this year springs from a bulb
that seems simple and compact, but within that bulb another bulb
is formed (or more than one) in the axils of the scales, which will
be the flowering bulb of next year; and within that is, again,
another bulbil, which will be the flowering bulb of the year after
next; so that each bulb lives three years, and no more, yet each, as
it comes to maturity, contains within itself other formed bulbs for
two years to come. Madame de Genlis, who wrote on almost every
subject in the beginning of the century, carries this still further,
and says that in October there will be found at the base of the bulb
the entire tulip flower which will appear aboveground in April,
with stem, petals, stamens, pistil, ovary, and seeds; but Madame
de Genlis is not to be trusted in her botany or her facts. But the
structure of the spring bulb which I have mentioned is a certain
fact, and, as far as I know, this structure is unique and confined to
the tulips, though there is something very analogous to it in the
structure of ferns. If a fern, of which the fronds of this year are
fully developed, is examined (in a large fern, such as the
Struthiopteris or *Felix mas*, it can be seen very easily), the fronds of
this year form the fine outside crown, but inside that there is an
inner crown of fronds a few inches high, but with each frond
separate and curled up, which will be the outside fronds of next
year, and within that, again, is a third ball of fronds not yet
separate, and with the points all tucked into one common centre,

and these will be the outside fronds of the year after next. I will finish this long account of the tulip by saying that though it must have been known to the Greek and Latin writers, it has not been found possible to identify it with certainty with any plant named by them. Its present name was given by Gesner in the sixteenth century, being the name of the Dalmatian hat, or cap, which the reflexed tulip was thought to resemble.

The tulip has led me too far astray, and left me little room to speak of the other flowers of May. I am much pleased this year with *Genista Andreana,* which flowered sparingly when young, but now bears an abundance of flowers. It is certainly a most desirable new plant, and is perfectly hardy, as we might expect from a plant of which one parent is our common broom, if, indeed, it is not a mere variety of the wild plant. I am surprised that it should do so well here, for the wild broom seldom grows well on lime, and so I do not attempt it. After flowering, my plant showed signs of withering, which I at first thought might arise from the drought; but, seeing it laden with seed-pods, I concluded that it had flowered too freely, and that if allowed to perfect its seed it would die, so I hardened my heart and cut it back very hard, and the bush very soon recovered. I think it is not sufficiently known that all flowering shrubs are much improved by being cut back after flowering and before they go to seed. By this means the strength of the plant is not wasted by perfecting the seeds, but is spent in laying up nourishment for next year's flowers. And this applies to all flowers, and may be seen most clearly in bulbous plants, which, after flowering, naturally produce seed-pods, but not on all the flowering stems. Those stems which do not produce seed-pods very soon fade away; those which are ripening seed will keep green and flourishing till the seed is formed, but if the seed-pods are cut away the flower-stem at once begins to die down, and the vital strength which would have been spent on the seeds remains stored up in the roots.

There are many other species of the broom family besides *Genista Andreana* which are beautiful ornaments in any garden, but I am inclined to give the palm to *G. virgata*, a shrub of very elegant growth, with small leaves, and an abundance of pale yellow flowers, and perfectly hardly, though its native home is in

Madeira. There are also many dwarf prostrate species, which make excellent plants for the rock-garden, but the family is too large for me to stay longer with them.

It is a pleasant puzzle to think what will be the effect of the long spring drought in the late summer and autumn garden. I have no doubt that one result will be to give an increased value to the summer bedding plants, for the ordinary plants of summer and autumn must pass away early, and then the 'bedders' will be useful, and I should think it very probable that many of the spring plants, which lasted so short a time and passed away so early, will flower again in the autumn. Another result which I look forward to with hope is, that many shrubs which often cannot ripen their fruit before the frost comes, and in some seasons cannot even flower, on account of the shortness of the summer, will be able to do so this year, when the summer may well be said to have begun in April. I mentioned last month that the Japanese orange, *Citrus trifoliata*, was in beautiful flower in April; it now has plenty of well-formed fruit, and, as in former years I have never seen the fruit formed before the end of summer, I may hope this year to see the fruit fully ripen.[1] For the same reason I hope to see flowers and fruit on the fine *Asparagus verticillatus* (already a beautiful green pillar quite fifteen feet high), on the Japanese Tchi-Tchi (*Diospyros costatus*), on the Christ's thorn, on the magnolias, and even perhaps on the *Smilax*, on the *Nandina*, and the *Periploca Græca*. I hope it may also ripen the golden pods of the Japanese *Kohlreuteria*, and the long pods, like French beans, of the *Catalpa*, both of which I had in the Jubilee year, but never before or since; and it surely must ripen the wood of our shrubs and fruit-trees, which will help them to withstand a hard winter, if it should be our ill-luck to add another hard winter to the three already past. If the long drought of March, April, and May brings us these results, we may not altogether regret it; and such results would go far to compensate for the trouble and anxieties which marred the pleasures of those eleven weeks of bright sunshine, and will also make some very memorable additions to my records of 'A Gloucestershire Garden.'

[1] It produced an abundance of small, handsome fruit, full of good seeds, which germinated freely.

CHAPTER VI

JUNE

Irises—Lilies—Roses—*Œnothera—Funkias—Honey-dew—Philadelphus—*
Ferns—A long drought

JUNE is the fullest month of the year in the garden, fullest in foliage and flower; it is Shakespeare's 'foison of the year.'

The chief flowers of June are the irises, the roses, and the lilies. Of the irises, the grand *I. ochroleuca* is one of the most stately, and is most ornamental. Its native country is not certainly known, but it has been a favourite in English gardens for more than a hundred years, and is said to have been brought from the East by the great traveller, Dr. Pococke, but there is no record of its having been found in a wild state. The most beautiful iris with me in the dry year of 1893 was *I. monnieri*, a very near relation of the Himalayan *I. aurea*, and generally in flower in July, but in that year quite a month before its usual time, and with flowers larger and purer in colour than I remember it before; so I suppose the drought and bright sunshine suit it well. *I. aurea* did fairly well, but instead of the flower-stems being over five feet high, as they often are in other seasons, they were not above a yard in height. But I do not think the drought will ever seriously injure the irises; by their premature flowering, and their small flowers which soon pass away, a very small tax is laid upon their vital powers, and they will probably be enabled to lay up a good store of strength for future years.

Of roses and lilies I cannot say much.[1] But there is no finality about roses; and when we remember the large number of books which have been written on them, and which every year adds to, I may plead that the subject is not exhausted. I have lately learned an additional excellence in the Banksia rose, which I had not noted before, that it lasts in flower longer than any other rose,

[1] See the chapters on 'Roses' and 'Lilies,' in Part II. Much of this June record was peculiar to the excellent summer of 1893, and I have abridged it accordingly.

except the monthly roses. I picked a good bunch on April 2nd; and on June 3rd there were still good bunches on the trees, though beginning to fade. I have also learned that the Himalayan *R. polyantha*, which is like a fountain of flowers, has a really unpleasant scent at times; so that, unlike other roses, which 'are fast flowers of their smells; so that you may walk by a whole row of them, and find nothing of their sweetness; yea, though it be in a morning's dew' (Bacon), this rose gives out its scent of its own accord for many yards round, and to me the scent is unpleasant. I know of only one other rose that can be called ill-scented, the Austrian briar, and in that the scent is not very perceptible; most of the modern hybrid roses have no scent at all, which in a rose is almost unpardonable. A very pleasant book has been recently published in France by M. Charles Joret, which is well worth reading by any lover of roses, for its exhaustive account of the classical and mediæval history of the rose; indeed, he carries it still further back, for he quotes from one of the old miracle plays on the Creation a speech of the Tempter, in which—'Le diable voulant dépeindre la nature délicate et fragile d'Eve, la compare à la rose:—

> 'Tu es fieblette et tendre chose,
> Et ce plus fresche que n'est rose.'

This must be the earliest instance of the degradation of the rose for the grossest flattery. Milton ventured to plant the rose in Paradise, but of a special sort, 'without thorn the rose'; but he has a touching allusion to the flower, in singling it out as one of the great losses which had come to him through his blindness:—

> 'With the year
> Seasons return, but not to me returns
> Day, or the sweet approach of ev'n or morn,
> Or sight of vernal bloom or summer's rose.'

The old rose Lamarque deserves a grateful record. It has always been a great favourite with me, and when in its full beauty I think it almost the most beautiful of white roses. I do not know its exact history, except that it is a tea-scented Noisette (which was a hybrid between *R. Indica* and *R. moschata*), and is the parent of the

Grand Cloth of Gold Rose, but it is not a popular rose, for it is not considered a good exhibition rose, and at the Rose Conference in 1889 it only obtained two votes as against nearly eighty for some of the other tea roses, for it has the reputation of being rather tender, which I very much doubt, my plant having been in the same place for certainly over fifty years, during which it must have passed through many a severe winter with little injury.[1] Its numerous trusses of pure white sweet-scented roses are most beautiful, especially in dry seasons; and if I were limited to one white rose I think I should choose Lamarque. The old white cabbage is also a great beauty.

The drought has more effect on the bulbous and herbaceous plants than it has upon the trees and shrubs. But I note two families of herbaceous plants which in my soil seem to rejoice in the drought, the œnotheras and the funkias. The œnotheras, or evening primroses, are beautiful plants, but I never could understand Linnæus's reason for giving this name, which he got from Theophrastus and Pliny, to a family of plants which are entirely American, though two have been admitted into the European and English floras, but there can be no doubt that they are aliens and garden escapes. Theophrastus's œnothera (*Vini venator*) is supposed to have been a willow herb, but Pliny's cannot be identified with any plant now known:—

'It is,' he says, 'an hearbe good as wine to make the heart merrie. It groweth with leaves resembling those of the almond-tree, and beareth flowers like unto roses. Of such virtue is this hearbe, that if it be given to drink to the wildest beast that is, it will tame the same and make it gentle.'—*Holland's Translation*.

The best known of the low-growing evening primroses is probably the old yellow *Œ. missouriensis*, and that is a plant that no garden should be without. But still more beautiful is the *Œ. caespitosa*, from the Rocky Mountains; every evening in June it will open many of its beautiful, pure white flowers, large and sweet scented, but soon fading away in the next day's sun; yet if they are picked and put in water they will preserve their beauty for some days. The *Œ. speciosa*, a very hardy plant from North America, is taller than the other two I have named, which are both prostrate

[1] In the hard winter of 1895 the Lamarque was less injured than most roses.

plants, but bears an abundance of white flowers, which do not confine their beauty to the evening and night, but keep themselves well open all the day; in some soils it is apt to become troublesome by spreading too much. For the funkias a dry season is most favourable; their great enemies are the snails and slugs, but the dry weather keeps these at bay. I admire the funkias very much; they like my soil, and grow into large plants; but I seldom succeed in flowering the beautiful *F. grandiflora* from Japan, and I believe the only way of getting it in full beauty is to grow it under glass.

A dry season is a favourable season for trees and well-established shrubs. Trees are very full-foliaged, and the flowering trees are laden with flowers. The tulip-tree is quite a sight with its load of pretty, sweet-scented flowers; the ashes are weighed down with their 'keys', and the limes are equally weighted with their flowers. But, besides flowers, some of the trees show such an extraordinary amount of honey-dew that it is almost unpleasant to walk under the lime-trees. This honey-dew is still something of a mystery. We know that it is in some way produced by innumerable aphides, and that the bees gather it, not for honey, but for bee-food. To the old writers it was a subject of much speculation. Virgil spoke of '*Aërii mellis coelestia dona,*' and '*Quercus sudabunt roscida mella.*' Pliny and other writers spoke of it positively as a falling dew from heaven, while the old English writers were more inclined to look on it as a sweet exudation from the earth and flowers; but of its usefulness to bee-keepers they had no doubt, and Butler, the most amusing of all the old writers on bees, says that—

'The hooni-dews fall' [his curious book is all printed phonetically] 'for the most part in the morning before it bee ligt; and then sall you hav the bees up in the morning as soon as they can see, making such a humming noys wer they go (specially in the garden, cooming loaden hom) that, as merry gossips wen they meet, a man may hear them farther than see them.'—BUTLER, *Feminin Monarchi*, 1636, vi. 44.

Of other shrubs I need only make mention of the *Philadelphus*, or mock orange. This is the shrub that is commonly called the syringa, and is so well known for its rich, almost overpowering orange-like scent, and the cucumber-like taste of the leaves. The common name, syringa, is a curious example of the way in which common names once established refuse to give way to more scientific arrangements. For under the one name of syringa the old writers, Clusius, Gerard, Parkinson, and others, lumped together both the mock oranges and the lilac, deriving the name from the Greek συριγξ, a pipe; '*a virgarum rectarum longitudine, et fungosae interioris medullae copia qua exempta ramuli fistulosi sunt*' (Clusius). Hence the old English name of pipe-tree, now lost. But botanically the mock orange and the lilacs are far apart, the lilacs being closely allied to the olives, while the mock oranges are near to, though quite distinct from, the myrtles, and so Linnæus separated them, calling the lilacs syringa, and giving to the mock oranges the old Greek name of *Philadelphus*, which is by many supposed to have been the jasmine. But a common name is not so easily thrown off, and to this day the mock oranges are commonly called syringas. There are many species, the chief favourite being the large North American *P. Gordonianus*, and this has the same scent as the common European *P. coronarius*, a scent which is too powerful to many except in the open air:—

'Of a pleasant, sweet smell (says Gerard), but in my judgment they are too sweet, troubling and molesting the head in a very strange manner. I once gathered the floures and layd them in my chamber window, which smelled more strongly after they had been together a few houres, with such an unacquainted savor, that they awaked me out of sleepe, so that I could not rest till I had cast them out of my chamber.'

Much as I admire these large-flowered mock oranges, I more admire the *P. hirsutus* from Tennessee; it has much smaller flowers, and they are not so sweet-scented, but they are produced in great abundance, and stud the branches in a particularly elegant way, and they are not so overwhelmed with the leaves, which are also small. And there is no better shrub for the rock-work than *P. microphyllus*; it comes from New Mexico, but it is remarkable for its low growth, its very small leaves, and its abundance of small flowers, which, however, are not produced till the shrub is some years old. A very near ally of the *Philadelphus* is the *Deutzia*, of which there are many species, chiefly from Japan, very hardy, and this year very full of flower.

It must be confessed that a long drought brings some trouble to the gardener, especially in new gardens, or where plants of any sort have been recently planted. In those cases the necessary constant use of the waterpot adds largely to the labours of the garden, and even so the plants may die; for plants require not only moisture at their roots, but also a moist atmosphere above them. We may have also to lament for the dwindled specimens of many of our flowers, fruit, and vegetables; but when we have said all that, and said it as grumblingly as possible, there surely is much in a hot dry season not to grumble at, but to rejoice and be thankful for. It is something to say, and it will be something to remember for many years, that throughout all England we have been able—for three continuous months[1]—to be out of doors in our gardens and fields under perfectly cloudless skies, with no fear of rain, with very little wind, and even with so little dew, that in the early mornings and in the late and long evenings the most delicate might sit out and enjoy the abundance of flowers (bright though short-lived), the rich scents of the pure air, and the sounds of the birds and insects, to whom the bright season seems to have brought a large addition of life and happiness. Nothing is absolutely perfect in this world (according to our ideas), and whatever the season may be there will be found some occasion for grumbling. But the wise man's conclusion is the best, *Omnia fecit pulchra in tempore suo*.

[1] Referring to 1893.

CHAPTER VII

JULY[1]

Xanthoceras sorbifolia—Syrian Oak—Eryngiums and their allies—*Gypsophila paniculata*—Spring flowers in autumn—Tenacity of plant-life

ONE of the best flowering shrubs for July is *Xanthoceras sorbifolia*. I have had this for many years, and it has frequently flowered here, but never fruited. Both in flower and fruit it is a most handsome shrub; indeed, when it was first sent to me from the *Jardins des Plantes*, in Paris, it came to me with the note that it was the best of all the flowering shrubs. I should be slow to pass that judgment upon any shrub, but it is very beautiful; yet, though perfectly hardy, it is very seldom seen. It is one of the many good things that were sent to France from Northern China by the Abbé David in 1868; it has rich green leaves something like the leaves of the ash, and the fruit is as large as an apple, and of a deep green; it is closely allied to our wild bladder nut (*Staphyleia*), and the horse-chestnuts, and it gets its name of Xanthoceras, or Yellowhorn, from the curious yellow horn-like glands placed between the stamens. In the July of 1893 the Mentone Asparagas (*A. acutifolius*) was also in full flower for the first time, and the Cochineal Oak (*Q. pseudo-coccifera*) produced abundance of acorns; these I had seen before, but they generally are formed too late to come to perfection. This interesting oak is very seldom seen in gardens; indeed, I have never seen it in England but at Kew and in my own garden; yet it is a very hardy evergreen, and forms a good bush, and is by no means a rare plant in its native countries; for it has a very wide geographical range, stretching from Spain to beyond Syria. Abraham's Oak at Mamre is of this species, and it is so abundant in Syria, that, according to Sir Joseph Hooker, who published a most interesting account of the oaks of Syria from personal observation in 1860—'On Mount Carmel it forms nine-tenths of the shrubby vegetation, and it is almost equally abundant on the

[1]This chapter, like the last, was written in the dry summer of 1893.

west flanks of the Anti-Lebanon, and many slopes and valleys of Lebanon.' The acorns on my tree are never larger than peas, but in Syria they are larger than any English acorns.

The drought of that year was also very favourable to all that large tribe of plants which many people despise, and lump them all as '*thistles*'; I mean not only the thistles proper (*carduus, cnicus, carlina*, etc.), but also the globe thistles (*echinops*), the teasles, and the eryngiums. I like them all, and grow many of them, and think that there are few finer herbaceous plants than the eryngiums when they are well established, and when the season suits them. There is a very great variety among them, from the silvery little *E. glaciale*, not more than two or three inches high, from Spain, to the tall species, *E. Oliveriarum*, with the handsome flowers borne on pale or deep-blue stems and involucres; and where this colour is well developed there is no other blue flower that can surpass it; but I think the colour is very dependent on soil and weather. There are many other pretty species, with very handsome foliage; and we have two British species—the Sea Holly, *E. maritimum*, common all round our coasts, with leaves that in some cases might almost be called blue, and which perhaps formed Sir John Falstaff's Eryngoes, for in his day the roots were candied and much liked, but which I do not remember to have seen grown successfully in gardens; while the *E. campestre* is easily grown, and even may become troublesome, but it is doubtfully native, though found in a few places. But I suppose the handsomest of all the Thistle family is the globe artichoke, *Cynara scolymus*, a native of Southern Europe, grown in England for more than three hundred years, generally in the kitchen-garden; but I have sometimes seen single plants grown on lawns with wonderful effect; and I well remember that the late Miss Marianne North had one on her lawn at Alderley (I think it is shown in one of the pictures in the North Gallery at Kew), which she had planted in a conspicuous position near the house, as one of the most decorative plants she could place there. I grow, and like for its curious appearance, a thistle that looks very like a dwarf globe artichoke; this is the *Carlina acanthoides*, with large deep-green leaves lying quite flat on the ground, and in the centre without any visible stem a flower looking very like an artichoke head cut off and dropped among the leaves; it has not much beauty, but is attractive from its curious appearance. All these thistles, if I may so class them all together, do exceedingly well in a dry year; the blue ones especially come of a richer and more metallic blue, and the luxuriance of this particular tribe is interesting by helping us to understand how it is that the dry desert parts of Eastern countries abound in thorny and prickly plants to the exclusion of many others. All travellers in the Syrian deserts have specially noted this, and there can be no doubt that the thorny thistly character of these plants is a great protection to them against browsing animals, for they mostly come into flower after the herbage is dried up, and if not so protected would very soon be destroyed.

The drought seems also to be very acceptable to another plant of a very different family, the *Gypsophila paniculata*. I have grown it for many years; and there is no plant which is so suggestive of a mist hanging over the plant. In this respect it is even superior to the wig-tree (*Rhus cotinus*), for in that the feathery, mist-like bunches are interspersed with the foliage, but in the gypsophila the little foliage does not show, and the whole plant is covered and surrounded with the mist. The plant is quite hardy, and comes from Austria and other parts of Central Europe. I first saw it, or first appreciated its beauty, at a flower-show held many years ago at a meeting of the Agricultural Society at Oxford. It was used in the prize bouquets, and it gave a lightness to them beyond any grasses; and for that purpose I have grown it ever since. The individual flowers are very small and inconspicuous, but they make a mass unlike any other plant; and though the name gypsophila points to its love of chalk, it will grow anywhere. The statices, or sea lavenders, seem also to rejoice in the drought, and this is not to be wondered at, for though they grow in places where the atmosphere is moist with sea-spray, they are often found among the rocks where there is the smallest amount of soil. There are many species, and all handsome plants which remain in flower a long time, and if picked before they are quite faded they may be kept all through the winter. Most of them are hardy, though there are some, perhaps the handsomest, from the Canary Islands, which can only be kept in the greenhouse. Linnæus took the names of *Statice* and *Limonium* from Pliny, though I should think it certain that Pliny's plants were in no way related to our sea lavenders; the older writers classed them amongst the *caryophylli*, or gilliflowers, and we still keep a remembrance of that in the name of sea pink for the armeria or thrift, which is so closely allied to the sea lavender that botanically it only differs by having its flowers in a close head instead of in a spike. The statices and armerias are found throughout the whole of the northern hemisphere as high north as the Arctic Circle, and there are nearly a hundred species, of which we have five in Great Britain.

But though the drought may be favourable to some plants, it is very unfavourable to others. The tall campanulas of all sorts are quite a failure; yet the platycodons, so nearly allied to the campanulas, do well; and all the low-growing campanulas, many of which are down plants, are also very bright and full of flower. The gentians are all rather stunted in growth; the *G. asclepiadea*, which is sometimes quite four feet high here, does not in a dry year exceed two feet, and I am surprised that it should suffer at all from drought, for in its native Swiss habitats it is often found in places exposed to the full sun and in shallow soils. I am not surprised that the saxifrages suffer, for most of them are lovers of wet places; but I am surprised that the sedums and sempervivums suffer, for they are all succulent plants, having in themselves a store of moisture which generally seems sufficient for all their wants, even when growing in the barest and driest spots, with little or no soil; yet many of them have shown that they feel the drought severely by curling themselves up into small balls, and so remaining till the rains come, when they again unfold themselves. I was also puzzled with the bamboos. Looking on them as sun-loving plants, I had not before fully realised how necessary moisture is to them; but up to the middle of July, though they showed no signs of distress, they scarcely sent up a single fresh shoot, when in other years the shoots of the year would have reached ten feet or more.[1]

The larger trees, such as oaks, elms, ashes, etc., are in wonderful luxuriance, and the drought seems to have no effect upon them; but I fancy this is owing not so much to their liking the long

[1] It is now found that the requisites for the successful growth of bamboos are abundance of manure and abundance of moisture.

bright sunshine, as to their having laid up last year a large supply of strength, which has enabled them to enjoy the sunshine without injury. The catalpa has flowered much before its usual time, for I have known years in which there was not even a leaf on the catalpa in the first week of July. It comes from North America, and I believe the name is the native Indian name of the tree; and the kœlreuteria, which comes from China and Japan, is equally hardy, and in July is covered with the curious bunches of flowers.

On the whole, after reckoning up all the losses and disappointments, I do not think that the gardener has much cause to complain of a long drought. There will be losses, of course, and so, perhaps, many gaps in the garden, but these we must expect every year from many causes, and the drought may teach us some good lessons. It teaches us very forcibly how steadily plant-life goes on in spite of all hindrances. It is really sad to go round the garden during a long drought, with the lawn brown, the shrubs getting scorched, and the beds looking almost like dust-heaps. Yet no sooner does the rain come than all is at once changed, and we are taught that the garden was by no means dead, but only biding its time; it was like a man who from illness or other cause is driven into enforced idleness, but who, as soon as the cause is removed, shows that the idleness was only from temporary weakness, which ended in increased strength. Within a very few days after the rains come to us after a long drought the grass becomes of the freshest green and the shrubs put out fresh leaves, herbaceous plants begin to shoot upwards, and it is no exaggeration to say that all Nature rejoices. I think none of us are aware what a large reserve of plant-life Nature is always keeping in the most unlikely places. We see it in our dust-heaps and ballast-heaps, which, left to themselves, soon get covered with vegetation; and I was told recently by an officer who had served at Suakim, that the tents of the soldiers were pitched in the barest sand of the desert, and that his tent was pitched next to the photographer's; and in a very few days the space between the two tents was clothed with a rich herbage, which sprang up from the water flung away by the photographer in washing his utensils. I think this lesson of the fixed certainty that with no real change, though with occasional short interruptions, the order of life goes steadily on, is a very valuable one. And it was a lesson which Henry Vaughan, the Silurist, who was a keen observer of Nature, and in some respects even surpassed George Herbert in seeing good in, and drawing good lessons from, the commonest objects in everyday life, has brought out in his poem on 'Man', in which he moralised on the changeableness of man as compared with the unchangeableness of Nature, and from which I will quote one stanza:—

> 'The flowers,
> Early as well as late,
> Rise with the sun, and set in the same bowers;
> I would (said I) my God would give
> The staidness of these things to man; for these
> To His Divine appointment ever cleave,
> And no new business breaks their peace.'

That is not the only lesson that may be learned from the long drought, producing a short appearance of desolation, and ending in the full beauty of fresh life and luxuriant vegetation; but I must not allow myself to moralise further, or to turn my Gloucestershire garden into a pulpit.

CHAPTER VIII

AUGUST

Box—White-leaved plants—Poles for climbers—Fuchsias—Hibiscus

THE garden record for August is very much the same as the record for July; but in the dry season of 1893 seeds and fruits were formed on many plants and shrubs which generally are not produced at all, or, if produced, come too late for ripening. Among these unusual fruits were the curious fruits of the common box-tree, and they are very curious, and well worth observing. For the box belongs to the great family of the Euphorbias or Spurges, a family which consists of more than 2500 species, and is spread all over the world, but which in Great Britain is confined to nine species of spurges, two species of dog's mercury (*Mercurialis*), and one species of box. The affinity of the box with the spurges is not very apparent when we compare our common box with the spurges which are such troublesome weeds in our flower-borders, but when the box shows its fruit the relationship is more easily recognised.

One result of long drought, followed by much rain is a wonderful and very rapid growth of luxuriant foliage; geraniums which stood quite still during the drought become most luxuriant. There is a peculiarity in one class of plants which is worth noting. The drought has little or no effect on plants, whether herbaceous or shrubby, which have white or grey leaves; they go on growing as if the season was normal; indeed, they rather seem to like the drought. The plants I mean are not what might be called albinos, white varieties of green-foliaged plants, but they are plants with typically white leaves, such as many of the Achilleas, the Artemisias, many of the New Zealand shrubs, etc. How these should be able to stand the drought better than other plants, I cannot say; but we know that they are also able to stand against sea-breezes strongly charged with salt, for many of the seaside shrubs have white or grey foliage; and I remember once being at Weston-super-Mare the day after a very remarkable gale, which blew from the Bristol Channel with great force. For many miles inland all the hedges had their windward sides as if a fire had passed over them, and in Weston itself, where the sea had been driven over the gardens near the beach, all shrubs and other plants with green leaves were seriously injured, while all those with white or grey foliage were quite unhurt. I do not profess to explain this, and I have never seen it explained,[1] but it is a curious fact in plant-life, which was again brought to my memory by the different effects produced by the drought of 1893 on plants of different colours.

A few years ago I thought I could add to the capacities of my garden by the erection of tall poles of oak, upon which I would train creepers of different kinds, vines, clematis, roses, brambles, wistaria, etc., and I am very pleased at the result. Already several of the poles are well covered, and I have a sort of rudimentary pergola; and I have little doubt that I shall see them all soon covered, and they will make a very pleasant feature in the garden. But on a few I trained some climbing annuals, and I am well pleased with them. On one I trained fancy gourds, chiefly the snake gourds. The foliage is most beautiful, and the flowers being pure white are very striking; but I do not get many fruits, for, for some reason which I cannot explain, nearly all the flowers are males, and the few female flowers produce fruit which does not come to perfection. On another pole I have trained *Cobœa scandens*, a very old favourite. As a rapid-growing climber it has few equals, and its flowers, which are like large bells, green at first and then turning to a rich purple, are very ornamental, and when it reaches the latter stage the stamens, which before were well inside the flower, grow to a considerable length, protruding far beyond the flower, and twisting themselves in a curious way, for which it is very hard to give a reason. But it is as a climber that the cobœa is such an interesting plant. Darwin, in 1865, in his delightful paper 'On the Movements and Habits of Climbing Plants', which afterwards took a new shape in his larger book on *The Movements of Plants* in 1880, gave a long description of the

---

[1] The white colour of the leaves is *tomentum*; and Linnæus' rule was, '*tomentum servat plantas a ventis; gaudet saepius colore incano.*'—Phil. Bot., 163. viii.

movements of cobœa.[1] He studied it as 'an admirably constructed climber,' and there is probably no plant from which the method by which plants climb by their tendrils can be better learned. Each shoot ends in a very fine branched tendril which stands upright, and each branchlet ends in one or more very delicate claws. The tendril steadily revolves in a circle till it meets with something to which it can attach itself by the little claws. These claws seize upon any irregularities and fix themselves there most firmly, and then, as soon as the attachment is complete, the long tendril begins to contract itself into a corkscrew, or rather a double corkscrew (for the twists are always double and in different directions), until in a very few days the branch, which may have been several inches from the support, is drawn close up to it, and secured to it so firmly that I never knew a plant blown down by the strongest wind. Altogether it is a very pretty lesson in plant-life, and one that can be learned and followed with very little trouble.

In a good season the garden is full of flowers in August, many of which may have appeared before, but that does not make them less welcome now. Roses, for instance, seem not to tire in their production of flowers; and among the shrubs there are many that in this month are showing a wonderful wealth of bloom, such as the Japanese privets, the hibiscus, and the hardy fuchsias. A few years ago it was considered bad taste to admire a fuchsia; but I always valued them as very bright objects in the autumn garden, and I am told that they are again becoming fashionable. They are all American plants, except three which are found in New Zealand; they belong botanically to the same family as the evening primroses, and in the south of England, I believe, they all may be grown as hardy herbaceous plants, except, perhaps, the beautiful *F. triphylla*, which is a tropical species. They are evidently very fond of the neighbourhood of the sea; on the coasts of Devon and Cornwall they grow luxuriantly, and do not require cutting down in winter; and at Kirkwall in the Orkneys I have seen houses covered with them from the ground to the roof, with spaces cut out for the windows. The hardiest I find to be *F. discolor, F. macrostemma, F. Riccartoni*, and *F. globosa*. Of the Japanese privets

[1]See p. 200.

I need say nothing; there are many varieties, and they all make good flowering shrubs for the late summer, but the Hibiscus, or *Althæa*, is such an old favourite in English gardens that it deserves a little more notice. The *Hibiscus Syriacus*, or *Althæa frutex*, was brought to England at the beginning of the seventeenth century, and it was not considered hardy: 'In the winter it must be kept in a large pott or tubbe, in the house or in a warme cellar, if you would have them to thrive' (Parkinson). It is, however, perfectly hardy, and forms a handsome bush, and, where the soil suits it, there are few handsomer flowering shrubs. It seems to like my soil, for my plants are covered with handsome flowers, which remain on the bush a long time. The prevailing colour is purple of different shades, but the one I admire most is a single flower of the purest white, called by the gardeners *Totus albus*. The finest of the family is the North American *Hibiscus grandiflorus*; it is herbaceous, or rather must be treated as an herbaceous plant, and generally flowers too late in the autumn, and gets injured by the frost, but will flower in hot years. In its native country it is a marsh plant, but here it seems to prefer a sunny place and ordinary garden soil.

CHAPTER IX

SEPTEMBER

Abundance of flowers—Bedding out—Asters—Fruits and seeds—Apparent
waste of seed

THE summer having been especially favourable to growth, with
rain at intervals in abundance, but also with a very fair amount of
bright sunshine, the result is a September quite remarkable for
the rich, fresh green of the whole country, especially of the
gardens, and for an abundance of vigorous plant-life. We have
lost or put aside the old English word 'foison,' which even in
Shakespeare's time was passing away, and it would be useless
affectation to attempt to revive it; yet we really have no word which
exactly expresses the same idea—the idea of luxuriant growth in
tree and herb and flower, and restricted to vegetable growth,
almost the same as the Latin *uber*, though not exactly, for *uber* is
sometimes applied to other kinds of plenty; but Shakespeare's
'Earth's increase, foison plenty,' would well describe the appearance of our fields and gardens in this year's September.

There is as yet no lack of flowers, and of many kinds. The
summer 'bedders' are at their best; and to those who wish for
large masses of colour in August and September, nothing is so
useful or so effective as these summer 'bedders.' To me a
'bedded-out' garden gives little pleasure, and I see little beauty in
'carpet beds' and 'pincushion borders,' but the flowers which
compose these beds and borders have each their charm and
beauty, and we cannot do without them. I would not willingly be
without the sweet scent of the heliotropes; and I use largely
geraniums, calceolarias, and begonias, but I use them as single
plants to fill up many gaps, and to brighten up many an odd
corner, and for such purposes they are most useful, and do what I
ask of them most effectually. But there are plenty of fine flowers
besides the 'bedders.' The autumn roses have been very abundant and beautiful; some more beautiful than in their midsummer
bloom. The grand old rose *Souvenir de Malmaison* is never so

beautiful in summer as in autumn, so that it is quite worth while to sacrifice the summer blooms, and let it bloom in autumn only. Then there are the beautiful asters,—not the gay French asters, which I cannot admire, though their colours are sometimes very beautiful, but they are too stiff and formal, only a little better than zinnias, which I think quite ugly flowers; but by beautiful asters I mean the Michaelmas daisies, the glory of the autumnal garden, and very delightful for their attractiveness to butterflies. A large plant of the rich blue *Aster amellus*, covered with peacock butter-flies, is a common sight enough, but it is a sight to be thankful for. And of all autumn flowers there is none more beautiful than the white Japanese anemone, which increases wonderfully with me, but of which one cannot have too much; for indeed I think there is no more beautiful hardy flower, and none more useful, as it lasts a long time in flower, and, when cut, will retain its beauty in water almost longer than any other. And among flowering shrubs, besides the roses, there is the beautiful *Abelia Chinensis* from China, now a mass of blossom from top to bottom, many varieties of the Japanese privet, the *Althæas* or Hibiscus in many colours, and some of the shrubby spiræas.

But I must leave the flowers because I wish to speak more particularly of what is to me a great interest in September, and that is the fruits and seeds of the garden. By fruits I do not so much mean the edible fruits—apples, pears, peaches, etc.—but I mean what botanists call fruits, *i.e.* the vessels containing the seeds of any plant and the seeds themselves. In the whole range of botanical science I know of no subject which is so fascinating and so deeply interesting as the study of seeds, technically, I believe, called carpology; and at no time of the year can it be so pleasantly followed up as in the month of September, for the garden is full now of seed-vessels of all sorts, many of them highly ornamental, and all more or less full of interest. I pass by the rowans and the hawthorns, though they are now in great beauty, but I class them more among the wild trees of the hedgerows. In the garden the most ornamental tree is the large-leaved spindle-tree (*Euonymus latifolius*) when covered with its brilliant scarlet fruit. Our own wild spindle-tree is a very pretty tree in fruit, but the fruit is small and dull in colour compared with the large-leaved species. I wonder this tree is not more common. Though a native of the south of Europe, it is quite hardy, and was known and apparently grown by Gerard and Parkinson, but it is very seldom seen. The scarlet fruit opens in four parts, and shows the orange-scarlet seeds inside. When thus open it bears a very close resemblance to the biretta, and it has thus obtained its French name of *bonnet de prêtre*, its Spanish name of *bonete de clerigo*, and its Portuguese name of *birette de clerigo*. There is a variety with white seeds which is worth growing, but not so handsome as the red-fruited species. Then there are the rose hips, and among the many species of roses (there are about forty species, with many intermediate varieties) there is as much difference in the hips as in the flower and foliage; indeed, there is more, for there are many species which at first sight are very similar in flower and leaf, but are totally dissimilar in the hip. I know of no rose that is not beautiful as seen in full fruit; but there are three or four that stand out as specially to be noted. The Japanese roses (*R. rugosa*) are perhaps the most admired when in fruit, but the apple rose, which is only a large-fruited variety of the English *Rosa villosa*, is as beautiful. The hips of the *Rosa grandiflora*, which is apparently the Siberian form of our Burnet rose or Scotch briar, are of the deepest black; while the hips of the Indian *R. microphylla* are as large as those of the Japanese rose, but quite distinct. Here this rose grows well, and is beautiful in flower and foliage, but it will not ripen its fruit; whereas at Kew it produces abundance of fruit as large as small apples, and very sweet scented. But to enter into the endless variety of the shapes and colours of the seed-vessels of different plants would require a volume. I merely mention these to show that they are in many cases as pleasant to the eye of the casual observer as they are interesting subjects of thought to those who desire to look deeper into the mysteries of nature. That they are deeply interesting to many is quite certain, and their chief interest lies in their mystery, and so in our real ignorance about them. As a seed lies in our hand, or under our microscope, we may, perhaps, see something of its shape and colour, but its history is too marvellous for us fully to read, for it has a long history of the past, and as long a history for the future. As to the history of the past, the old idea that plants were created in order that fruits and other products useful and pleasant to man might be brought into existence, and for those purposes only, has long been exploded; and we now believe that the whole life of a plant is directed to the one object of forming seed for the continuance of the life of the plant. Not for the sake of the beautiful flowers has the plant gone through its life: the beautiful flowers themselves were only one step onward in the formation of the seed. To form that little seed the plant lay dormant through the cold of winter, and in due time sprang up from its winter's sleep; for the sake of that only stem and leaves were formed, and became the conduits of pure air and moisture, and carried the warmth of the sun and the refreshing rain to the root and sap which were gradually building up the wonderful architecture of the flower; for the sake of the seed only was the flower formed with calyx, corolla, pistil, stamens, and ovary, with colours and lines and scents to attract insects that would be friendly helps, or it may be with an equally subtle arrangement to ward off others that would be hurtful. That is something of the past history of the seed, but it has also a future history. That small object contains within itself a something which will develop into root, stem, leaves, flower, and seed, which will last for less than one year, perhaps as an annual, or for hundreds of years in a forest tree, according to the eternal law fixed upon 'every herb bearing seed which is upon the face of all the earth, and every tree in which is the fruit of a tree yielding seed.'

But though such care has been taken to produce and protect the seed, the apparent waste of seed is enormous and quite inexplicable. I mean that the number of living plants produced from every good seed bears no proportion to the amount of seed formed and ripened. In my own garden, for instance, there must be millions of seeds formed, and for the most part ripened every year; and yet, with the exception of such things as groundsel, thistle, and other garden weeds, which seem to have an un-bounded power of germination, it is very unusual to find any quantity of seedlings. It is the same with our common forest trees. Our common elm does not form seed; but what becomes of the thousands of seeds dropped from our oaks, ashes, limes, chest-nuts, etc.? Here and there we may find a solitary seedling, but that is all. Many are browsed away by sheep and cattle, and many are eaten by birds; but those are not all destroyed, for in many cases seeds germinate more readily after passing through the birds, but by far the greater number seem to be wasted. Still, I feel sure they are not really wasted, and there are curious instances how they will bide their time upon or under the ground till the fitting opportunity for their germination arrives. This has been often shown by the rapid appearance of young vegetation after forest fires, and there is a well-known experiment of Darwin's showing how full of latent life the earth is, which has been often quoted, but is worth repetition:—

'I took in February three tablespoonfuls of mud from three different points, beneath water on the edge of a little pond; this mud when dry weighed only 6¾ oz. I kept it covered in my study for six months, pulling up and counting each plant as it grew; the plants were of many kinds, and were altogether 537 in number, and yet the viscid mud was all contained in a breakfast cup.'—*Origin of Species*, 386.

There is one very curious point in seed-life which always seems to me a special puzzle. Plants seem to know (if I may say so) when they are going to die, and then to be able to put forth more vigorous means for their reproduction. All gardeners know some instances of this in some form or other, and in my own garden it has been brought before me this year in a very marked manner. For many years I have grown a pretty little sea lavender (*Statice Cosyrensis*) from Cosyra, a small island between Italy and Africa, now called Pantellaria. Though a free bloomer, I never knew it to produce a seedling or to form seed. Last year it showed signs of decay from old age, and it entirely disappeared in the winter, but this spring I found a flourishing young seedling about a foot from the parent plant, and since that I have found two or three more still farther away.

But I must come to a stop. I have only touched the fringe of the subject, but from the little I have said I hope my readers may learn that there is much beauty left in their gardens even when the flowers are faded. They will find the subject very puzzling and very mysterious, but also very full of interest, and not the less so because it will show how with all our knowledge of plants we still have much to learn, and indeed are very ignorant. It may interest any who take up the subject to note how often in the New Testament the mysteries of the kingdom of heaven are compared to the mysteries of seed-life, and how the Great Teacher Himself told us of man's ignorance on such a common everyday thing as the growth of a seed. 'Si homo jaciat semen in terram, et dormiat et exsurgat nocte et die, et semen germinet et increscat, *dum nescit ille.*'

CHAPTER X

OCTOBER

Skeleton leaves—*Cotoneaster*—Pæonies—Fuchsias—*Helianthus*—Asters—Ivy

THE modern description of October is 'chill October' or 'dull October'; the older description of the month was very different. To our forefathers October came

> 'Full of merry glee,
> For yet his noule was totty of the must
> Which he was treading in the wine vat's sea,
> And of the joyous yale whose gentle gust
> Made him so frollick and so full of lust.'—SPENSER.

To them it was the month which put the crown on the labours of the year, and they rejoiced in it accordingly. But to us who can no longer rejoice in a vintage, but may well be content with our harvest and with our hop-gathering, which is almost more beautiful than a vintage, October has its charms. It may have its cold and even frosty nights, which work sad havoc in the gardens, and it may have its cold, cheerless, and dull days; but it is not always so, and when we do get a bright, sunny October it is a most cheerful and pleasant time, and especially so, as I think, in the gardens.

Certainly a bright English October is full of pleasant sights in the garden. I spoke in my last chapter of the beauty and interest of the fruits and seed-vessels, which can be studied now better than at any other time, but I left so much unsaid that I must return to the same subject again. I am fond of a plant which is very hardy and, in some places, very common, but is almost unknown to many gardeners. This is the *Physalis alkekengi*, or winter cherry, of no great beauty in flower, but very handsome in fruit, and having two curious stages in its fruit, both of which have their separate beauty. The rather dull white flower is followed by what looks a handsome scarlet fruit. This, however, is only the remains of the calyx, but is more like a bladder than a calyx. If opened, a green fruit will be found inside, which is sometimes called the Cape gooseberry, and eaten; but the Cape gooseberry (*Physalis edulis*) is a pleasant and wholesome fruit, and may be easily grown in a cool greenhouse; whereas the winter cherry has a bad reputation, but I believe it to be quite harmless, though it comes of a suspicious family, the *Solanaceæ*. As the winter comes on the fruit enters on the second stage, and it is in this stage that I consider it most beautiful. The scarlet covering gradually disappears, and in its place is a sort of a cage of exquisite texture, from the top of the inside of which there drops a scarlet fruit of the size and colour of a cherry. The whole outside covering has become skeletonised and white, and how this is done naturally is a puzzle which I have never seen satisfactorily explained. We can easily skeletonise leaves and fruits artificially, but in the *alkekengi* this is done slowly, and apparently by the action of the atmosphere on the thin, pulpy portion of the fruit. Many leaves are skeletonised in the same way after falling from the trees, especially poplar leaves and the butcher-brooms, but I can only call to mind two other plants in which this skeletonising seems to be a regular part of the life of the plant. The little *Rubus australis* is the most southern bramble known, coming from NewZealand, and also, I believe, from the Falkland Islands; and one of its varieties has only skeleton leaves—*i.e.* it has only the midribs of the leaves, but these are set with small white thorns, which give the whole plant almost a jewelled appearance. It is easily grown, and is fairly hardy. But by far the most beautiful of these naturally skeletonised plants is the lace leaf of Madagascar (*Ouviranda fenestralis*), the leaves of which (to quote the botanical description in the *Bot. Mag.*) 'are constituted by a series of the most beautiful network, without parenchyma, reduced, in short, to its vascular reticulated tissue.' In more simple language, the long leaves are lovely specimens of natural lacework, but, of course, it is not hardy; it requires a tank in a hothouse, and if I had a hothouse I would certainly grow this. But the *alkekengi* is perfectly hardy, and on a small scale is as beautiful as the lace plant. It grows wild in many parts of Europe, but not in Great Britain. Its name seems to point to Arabia as another native habitat, and I suppose it grows in Japan, for it is described and beautifully figured in the wonderful Japanese book of botany, the *So moku*. It may, then, be grown anywhere; and I once saw a large bed of it in a vicarage garden in Berkshire, where it was grown for Christmas decorations; and perhaps this is the best way of growing it, in a bed by itself, for if grown with other flowers it is apt to become troublesome, 'the roots be long, not unlike the roots of Couch-grasse, ramping and creeping within the upper crust of the earth farre abroad, whereby it encreaseth greatly' (Gerard).

The *physalis* has detained me too long; at a much shorter length I must describe a few other fruiting shrubs which are now making bright spots in the garden. The low-growing *Cotoneaster horizontalis* from the Himalayas is a surprise to all who see it. It lies flat upon the ground, and the smaller branches radiate from both sides of the main branches with such wonderful regularity that they almost resemble the skeleton of a flatfish. It is not completely evergreen, but the young leaves appear very early in spring, and the whole plant is then covered with pretty red buds, which open into small white flowers, followed by a profusion of bright scarlet berries, which remain for a long time, and are a great ornament. At present the plant is rather scarce, but as it can be raised easily both from seeds and cuttings it will probably soon become common; and having grown it for some years I can strongly recommend it as one of the best shrubs I know for the low parts of a rockwork, or any other place well beneath the eye.

Then there are the barberries. Our common barberry is now considered a native of England, yet Turner, a good observer, writing in 1548, said of it: 'Barberries growe wylde in the hedges and woddes in Germany, but in Englande only in gardines'; and, though the name has a very English sound, it is really a corruption from the Arabic name. It once had an evil reputation as producing rust in wheat, but that idea is now exploded, and it may be grown without fear anywhere. Where it grows well its scarlet fruit makes a very pretty object in autumn; but it is capricious, and will not fruit everywhere; it does not fruit here well. The most beautiful variety is that in which the fruits have no seed inside (*B. asperma*), the fruits being both larger and more brilliant in colour than the more common sort. There are many other foreign species (about fifty in all), chiefly from China and the Himalayas, and a few are found in America. But of all the Berberids there is none, I think, to compare with *Nandina domestica*. As a decorative shrub it is very highly valued in China and Japan, and is there called the sacred bamboo, but, though it has been grown in England for nearly a hundred years, and is quite hardy, it is very seldom seen. Its great beauty is in the foliage, the leaves being very various both in colour and shape, and very graceful; the flowers are pretty and remain long upon the bush, and are followed by curious and handsome fruit, which, however, is seldom produced in England. It can be trained to a wall, or grown as a bush, and however grown is always attractive.

Among the fruits of October I must not omit the fruit of the pæony (*P. corallina*). I grow many pæonies, but I do not know of any that produce the handsome seed-vessels that this so-called British pæony produces. It is certainly not a British plant, and is now excluded from the British flora, but it has been naturalised for many years in the Steep Holmes in the British Channel; and its beauty consists in the two sorts of seeds, red and black, which are respectively the fertile and unfertile seeds:—

'The round black shining seeds, which are the true seed, being full and good, and many red or crimson grains which are lanck and idle, intermixed among the black, as if they were good seed, whereby it maketh a very pretty show.'— PARKINSON.

With a simple mention of the fruits of the thorn apple, both the common white (*Datura Stramonium*) and the purple (*D. Tatula*), not so handsome in flower, but more handsome in fruit, and both very old inhabitants of English gardens, I will leave the fruits and seeds of October, to say something about the flowers.

The swallows have quite left us, and we have had some sharp frosts, which have cleared away some of the tender summer flowers (begonias, heliotropes, dahlias, etc.), and, which I much more regret, have stripped the leaves from many of the trees while they were still green, and so have robbed us of much of our best autumnal-tinted foliage. The mulberry, the catalpa, the salis- buria, and many others, are in their bare winter form, and the brightness of the St. Luke's summer was sadly marred. Still we have plenty of flowers left. I am surprised at a fine bunch of

Alstraemeria psittacina, or *pulchella*, which has been in full flower for some weeks, and has been as yet uninjured by frosts. It is true that I have it in a very sheltered corner, but it is a Brazilian plant, and though I have grown it for many years in the same place I have not before noted it as a good flowering plant for the late autumn. The Pampas grasses are very late this year, and I suppose that arises from their starting into growth very late in the cold spring. The male Pampas grass will not flower at all this year, and the female was too late to be of use in harvest decorations; but its place was well filled by the bamboos, which have been in quite luxuriant growth this year. The hardy fuchsias, though rather late, have been very full of blossom, and they are shrubs which I value for their rich autumn blooming. I grow most of the hardy kinds, and have done so for many years, though I have been often told by friends who call themselves æsthetic that they have no beauty; I am therefore rather amused to see how they are again becoming fashionable. I have grown in the open ground in summer the beautiful new *F. triphylla*, and it has been a great success. I call it new because it was introduced into England less than ten years ago, yet it is really the oldest fuchsia known, having been discovered more than a hundred and fifty years ago, and being the plant on which the genus was founded. As it comes from the West Indies it will almost certainly not be hardy, but it grows readily from cuttings, and will make a lovely plant for the summer borders, as its beautiful waxy orange-scarlet flowers cannot easily be surpassed. And a most beautiful shrub for the late autumn is *Caryopteris mastacanthus*. It is a shrub about five feet high, now covered with a profusion of pale blue flowers. It is a native of Canton, and is considered to be rather tender; but in this part of England it appears to be quite hardy, and the leaves have a delicate and to me a pleasant scent. In its native country it is used in the manufacture of mastic, but I believe it does not enter into the mastic used in England, which is entirely produced from the European *Pistacia*. The perennial sunflowers have been, and still are, very good; and among them I like especially the *Helianthus giganteus*, a plant that in good soil will reach ten feet in height, and produce for many weeks an abundance of flowers of the purest yellow. As a North American plant it is very hardy, and is now becoming common. It seems to be very popular for the gardens of railway stations, in several of which I have seen it in great abundance. I also like the *H. orgyalis* from the Rocky Mountains, which is as tall as the other, and though the flowers are not so handsome, the habit of the plant is very graceful, the tall stems being clothed with long narrow leaves (sometimes sixteen inches long) which hang down, and give the plant almost a palm-like appearance. But the best flowers of October are still the Michaelmas daisies. Some have passed away, but those that remain are among the best, such as *Aster turbinellus*, *A. cordifolius*, and *A. mutliflorus*. But the bravest show is made by the two forms, blue and rose, of the *A. Novae Angliae*, which no weather seems to hurt, and which may be expected to keep in beauty almost till the middle of November, perhaps later. With me they are the latest of the asters, and so are specially prized, for I have never succeeded well with *Aster grandiflorus*, which I have sometimes seen in flower at Christmas, but which, coming from the Southern United States, is not so hardy as the others.

Passing a few steps outside the garden I come upon a mass of flowers which deserve a passing notice, and which shall be the last October flower that I will name. On the top of an old wall there is a thick covering of old ivy now laden with flowers. It is a good instance of the habit of the ivy not to flower as long as it is climbing, but as soon as it has reached its possible limit it breaks out into flower. I need say nothing to recommend the ivy in any form: it is a favourite with all, except with the late Professor Freeman, who disliked it for its interference with his views of ancient buildings, and had no better names for it than 'that baleful plant', 'that insidious weed', etc. Those who wish to know all about it should read Shirley Hibberd's pretty monograph on it; but I will resist the temptation to say more, for my chapter has already run to its full length. I must note, however, that we are still picking good roses,—the last survivors, but very sweet, and very acceptable.

CHAPTER XI

NOVEMBER

Outside gardens—Autumnal tints—Anatomy of trees—Removal of plants—
Changes in the garden—Growth of plants in November

WHEN Horace Walpole described the great changes in gardening which Kent had effected, he summed up his work in a happy phrase, which has almost become proverbial: 'He leaped the fence, and saw that all nature was a garden.' The discovery led the way to the modern landscape gardening, and to the destruction of the old English gardens, but I do not know enough of Kent to say whether this idea of the unbounded extent of gardens was to him any real pleasure. But I have never considered that my garden ended at the garden fence; I have many outside gardens in the woods and downs, the fields and hedgerows, and the rivers, and many also in my neighbours' gardens, in all of which I can enjoy, almost as if they were my own, many plants which it may be well to keep out of the garden proper, or which grow better elsewhere than with me. Thus, I would not be altogether without the wild bramble and the dog-rose, but I can see them better in the hedgerows; the creeping Jenny (now so popular in the hanging baskets and window-boxes of town gardens) grows abundantly for me in a near meadow; the grand white and yellow dead nettles would be a real ornament to my garden, but those, too, I prefer to keep in the hedgerows; the pretty quinsywort (*Asperula cynanchica*) will not grow in my garden, but I can always see it on the downs; nor can I keep for long the beautiful large butterfly orchis or the bee orchis, but I can at any time see them by walking to a wood not two miles away; while in another wood I can see the rare little *Gagea lutea*, and the curious parasitical toothwort (*Lathrea squamaria*); and, having no place for aquatics, I cannot grow the flowering rush or the water-lilies, but I am content to enjoy them in the river which bounds the parish. In the same way, I consider that I grow in my neighbours' gardens many plants that I cannot grow in my own. My low elevation forbids the growth of the high

Alpines, and even of such plants as the *Onosmas*, but they grow well in a neighbour's garden at a slightly higher elevation. I go to another neighbour's garden every spring to admire a grand display of Crown Imperials; and in many cottage gardens I admire (I hope without undue envy) the spikes of white lilies, which with me are very loth to flower at all.

But at no other time of the year is the value of these outside gardens more brought home to me than in the late autumn, in the end of October and the beginning of November. The elm is the common tree of this district, and as I look round my garden I am forced to acknowledge that the points of interest and beauty have been much diminished; but when I look at its surroundings and see the hillsides and hedgerows, which form a part of my garden view, a rich mass of golden foliage, I then see that the interest and beauty have only been changed from one part of the garden to another. I lately saw, in an American paper, an account of the beauty of the American autumn, in which this view of the extension of the garden is very pleasantly put:—

'At this time of year the garden seems to me the least interesting one of the year, . . . but around us is the glamour of the glorious American autumn, tinging the fields and ripening leaves with a wealth of colours overpowering the brightest garden. Seen under a declining sun at this season, our Jersey meadows show broad, harmonious, and exquisite shadings of colour, which no expert in bedding-out can hope to rival. When one has perceptions open to these impressions, the mere enclosed garden is at this season rather commonplace.'

Though I welcome these autumnal beauties, and claim them as parts of my garden, though outside the garden fence, I do not intend in this paper to speak of the beauties of autumnal foliage. But I must mention a North American sumach, which promises to be one of the most beautiful of our autumnal shrubs. This is the *Rhus cotinoides*, a native of Alabama, in the Southern United States, and apparently very rare there. It seems to be perfectly hardy, is deciduous, and forms a low bush. In the spring the leaves are a delicate rose colour, but early in autumn they become an intense crimson, richer than any Japanese maple, and remain on the bush in all their brilliancy for a long time. I have not seen the flowers, but they are small and inconspicuous, and I believe it has not yet flowered in England.

There is plenty of work in the garden in November, and in its way very interesting, the more so because it is unlike the work of any other month. We may lament the loss of leaves on the trees, and the change in them from thick masses of green to bare skeletons. But these skeletons have a beauty of their own, and to the botanist and student of tree-life they are a very pleasant study; indeed, no one can venture on a record of the life of a tree or shrub who does not as much study its anatomy in the winter as he does the leaves, flowers, and fruits in the summer. The anatomy of trees is a constant marvel, and to study it thoroughly will teach many unexpected lessons: to mark the different angles and thicknesses of the branches, varying in every tree according to the necessities of each family and each species, and varying in trees of the same species according to their position as regards light and soil and prevailing winds, will require many a winter's study. And in November, when the trees are bare of leaves, is the time for that pruning of trees which is one of the pleasantest labours of the garden, and one of the most healthy; but it is an art that is not soon learned, and in no branch of gardening does experience and steady observation of the wants and growth of trees produce better results. A tree that has been well looked after from its infancy will show a vigour both in girth and height over neglected trees that will be a surprise to many, and a good object-lesson to those who think that everything may be left to nature.

Another very pleasant November work is the carrying out alterations in the garden, including the removal of all sorts of plants. I am in the habit during the summer of making notes of work to be done in the winter, such as the removal of plants which are getting too crowded, or which are evidently not happy in their present position, or the alteration of paths and beds made necessary by the growth of trees, or it may be merely by the desire for change; and all such work is best done in November. In some gardens there is a great deal of work done in the separation of plants, and I know of many who think that frequent separation is absolutely necessary to the well-being of plants. It may be so in some soils, especially in heavy clay soils, but I am glad that it is not necessary for me. I find it better to leave plants alone as much as possible; there are some which from time to time I may be obliged to divide, but I do it unwillingly, for I find, in many cases, that it takes them more than a year to recover from the operation. This is especially the case with roses, lilies, and pæonies, but I believe this is entirely a question of soil, and what is a law for my garden is no law for others. In my own garden I am not afraid of moving plants at almost any time of the year, if I see the necessity for it; but to move plants in the height of summer requires extra care in planting, and much watching after planting; in November the work is much easier. There are few gardening works in which a gardener's skill, or want of skill, are more shown than in removing plants from one place to another, especially shrubs; and in no branch are there so many disappointments when the work is done by careless or unskilful hands. All that such trees or shrubs ask for is that they should be kept out of the ground as short a time as possible, and be placed in their new home very firmly; and, to get this firmness, a few heavy stones placed near the stem are a good help, they prevent the plant being much swayed by the wind, and they prevent the evaporation of moisture and the loss of warmth by radiation.

But it is not my object to give rules for gardening, I wish rather to record the work done in the month, so I must give a few lines to another garden work for which the month of November is very suitable. Every garden is subject to many changes; in each year trees and bushes grow, and call for more room; and then paths must be altered, and old beds, perhaps, destroyed, and new ones made. And I have always noticed that the more a man loves his garden, the more he delights in constantly changing the arrangements, which were, perhaps, good for a time. but which, as time goes on, must give way to others; and the most uninteresting garden is one that has been made on a fixed plan, rigidly adhered to through succeeding years, till what may have been good and beautiful at the beginning becomes dull, uninteresting, and ugly. Personally, I have little faith in fixed plans, perhaps because I have never had any plan in my own garden; such as it is, it has grown into its present shape and plan, and has almost formed itself; and I may say with certainty that though I have many trees, shrubs, and other plants which have been in their present places for many years—many over seventy years—yet there is not a single path or flower-bed that is the same now as it was thirty or even twenty years ago. And this adds much to the pleasure of a garden; this power of altering to suit the wants of growing trees and shrubs, or it may be only to suit one's own peculiar taste or fancy, gives a pleasant feeling of ownership which nothing else will give.

The month of November, then, is not all dull and dreary: there is no blaze of flowers, but there is much room for pleasant work, and, to those who know where to look for it, there is much interesting plant-life to observe. In a garden there is no such thing as absolute rest, though we talk as if there was.

> 'Each month is various to present
> The world with some development.'
> —*The Two Voices.*

And in November plant-life is really very active. It always seems to me a wonderful thing that in this month, when we are doing all we can to protect our favourites from the bitter frosts which we know will be with us shortly, nature is clothing many plants with young fresh leaves which must be, as we suppose, more or less tender. This is most seen in many of the herbaceous plants, which already have as many radical leaves as they ever will have, but it is seen also in many shrubs; and it is to me very remarkable that some tender shrubs put out their young leaves, while the hardier ones show no such signs of returning life. For instance, the beautiful fuchsia gooseberry (*Ribes speciosum*), from California and Mexico, is now showing its young green leaves, while our own hardy gooseberry shows none. There are many such instances, and I suppose in the *Ribes*, and probably in all the others, this early leafing is a reminiscence of the habits of the plants in their native countries. Then the daffodils are pushing their way through the ground; the buds of the Christmas roses are well formed; the catkins of the hazel are fairly abundant, and those of the *Garrya* are lengthening every day; while it is easy to find primroses in flower in many places, but I always suppose those to be the late flowering or double-flowering specimens of the present year, and not the premature flowers of next spring—however, they are very welcome.

'The primrose yet is dear,
The primrose of the later year,
As not unlike to that of spring.'
—*In Memorium.*

In the general absence of flowers in November, there is a special value in two shrubs, which in favourable soils are now in full flower. These are the laurustinus and the dwarf gorse. The laurustinus lives with me, but never flowers well; perhaps it does not like the abundance of lime in the soil, yet I know it in great beauty growing on pure oolite; but nowhere do I see it more flourishing or more covered with flowers than in one of my outside gardens on the red sandstone. It is nearly related to our guelder-rose and the wayfaring tree, but is not a British plant, though a very old favourite in English gardens. It comes chiefly from Southern Europe, but is quite hardy, except in the severest winters, when it gets cut down, but not killed; but when frosted the smell is most offensive and far-reaching. There is a variety with shiny leaves and large flowers (*V. lucidum*), which I have seen in the Isle of Wight and Devonshire, like large bushes of *Kalmia*, but it is rather tender. The dwarf gorse, *Ulex nanus*, seems also to like the sandstone formation. It is closely allied to the common gorse, but lies prostrate on the ground, and flowers in the autumn. It would be a good plant for low rockeries, but it might be troublesome, for I notice on our railway banks and cuttings that it spreads rapidly; yet where it can be watched it might be grown for its bright golden flowers, which would be welcome at any time, but are doubly welcome in November. It is not a very rare plant, but it is very local. I have not found it in many places, but I found it abundantly in the New Forest, and it grows on Wimbledon Common, but not abundantly.

Certainly the absence of sun, and the dull skies, do make November a dull and gloomy month; and I know that to many, and some of them lovers of gardens, the garden in November is a piteous object, and so saddening that they feel obliged to leave it for the seaside. I am thankful to say that to me it is not so; indeed, the seaside in November would be far more dispiriting to me than my own garden, with its bare trees and falling leaves, for I have no dislike to bare trees and falling leaves in their proper seasons. And it is curious to note how differently the same sights and smells of the late autumn affect different people. Tennyson, with all his love of a garden, records his feelings of the season—

> 'The air is damp and hushed and close,
>   As a sick man's room when he taketh repose
>   An hour before death—
>   My very heart faints and my whole soul grieves
>   At the moist rich smell of the rotting leaves,
>   And the breath
>   Of the fading edges of box beneath,
>   And the year's last rose.'

On the other hand, Mr. Bright, almost parodying this, says 'the air is soft and warm and still . . . there is an aromatic fragrance everywhere from the withering leaves and from the lingering flowers.' He is forced, however, to add, 'but there is sadness with it all,' and it is the only note of sadness in the *Year in a Lancashire Garden*. To a great extent I must agree with him. November, especially the latter part of it, is not a bright month in the garden, in some respects it is more gloomy even than December; but with all its dulness and gloominess I hold that it has an interest and even a beauty of its own. And I am glad to say that I am not alone in my appreciation of the garden in November, for among the ornaments of the garden I now reckon the starlings. They have been away for some months, but are now coming back to us. What they find on the lawn I do not exactly know, but they are very busy, and apparently very happy, and I admire them much, and gladly welcome them.

CHAPTER XII

DECEMBER

Bowles's *Flora*—Conifers—Variegated shrubs—Ferns—Laurustinus—Looking forward—Conclusion

WHAT can any one say of the garden in December? Can any one honestly say that a garden in December is pleasant, or can give pleasant thoughts? The general verdict of December would be given in Tennyson's words:—

> 'Earthward he boweth the heavy stalks
> Of the mouldering flowers;
> Heavily hangs the broad sunflower
> Over its grave i' the earth so chilly;
> Heavily hangs the hollyhock
> Heavily hangs the tiger-lily.'

And, as Tennyson is speaking of 'the year's last hours,' he evidently was not in the habit of making things neat in the garden by cutting down the old flower-stems. If that was his habit I am much inclined to agree with him; I never think that the prospect of the garden in December is much better by making all the flower-beds too tidy. I feel sure that the dead flower-stems (the 'Kecksies' of Shakespeare and the old writers, and the word still lingers in a few parts) must be some protection to the plants; and, when the hoar-frosts come, these dead stems, especially where the dead flower-heads remain, put on a wonderful beauty, as any one may see who will walk by an old hedgerow in a hoar-frost and look at the rank herbage, particularly where there is any abundance of the large umbelliferous plants.

But even in December the garden is not altogether without flowers, and, as wise Ulysses says, 'Though much is taken, much abides.' About a hundred years ago a pretty book was published called Bowles's *Flora; or, a Curious Collection of the most Beautiful Flowers as they appear in their Greatest Perfection each Month of the Year.* There are twelve plates, one for each month; and in each is a vase filled with the flowers of the month. They are well drawn and engraved, and coloured by hand; and it was a very popular book, for in old houses I have often seen the set of plates framed and glazed. The flowers have all their English names, and it is easy to see that our grandfathers could in each month show collections of flowers which were as beautiful as those we have now, though perhaps not so varied. In the plate for December the vase holds thirty-six different flowers. Of these, a few are greenhouse flowers, and some are clearly out of season, though in some seasons they may be gathered in December; but the list of the hardy flowers is sufficiently interesting to be worth copying. They are auricula, pansies, white corn marigold, strawberry daisy (a very double sort), laurustinus, red spring cyclamen (*C. coum*), Christmas flower (Helleborus niger), winter white primrose, gentianella, yellow corn marigold, valerian, winter double crowfoot, St. Peter's shrub (a white-flowered shrub which I cannot identify), mountain avens, single anemone, sage and rosemary, winter flowering pear (I suppose the Gloucester pear, which, like the Glastonbury thorn, often flowers in December), Spanish Virgin's bower (evidently from the leaf *Clematis cirrhosa*, but the artist had not seen the flower, and imagined it incorrectly), Glastonbury thorn, and buds of monthly rose. This is really a goodly list, and no doubt they might all be gathered in December, but not all at the same time, and most of them I could gather here, but not all. We had our first snow on December 4th, and the day before I got my first true Christmas rose, by which I mean to exclude the fine *Helleborus altifolius*, which can more often be gathered in October than December. I never saw the white corn marigold, and I carefully keep out of my garden the corn marigold, for it is a dreadful weed, and if it were to escape out of my garden into the cornfields the farmers would have good reason to condemn my garden as a public nuisance. But I have been much astonished to see the common marigold holding its beauty so late; not only in my own garden, but in many neighbouring gardens it has been in quite its summer brightness till past the middle of December. I do not think this is out of the common, but it had certainly escaped my notice in former years. A shrub that can show in December a mass of blossoms as golden as the marigold is the yellow Chinese jasmine (*J. nudiflorum*), certainly a great ornament where it can be well grown, and it covers many cottages in my village, but I never very much admired it. The leaves fall very early in the autumn, and then there is nothing to conceal the stiff angular growth of the plant (it was first called *J. angulare*); yet the individual sprays are bright and pretty, and if grown as a bush much of this ugly habit is concealed.

But though there is no abundance of flowers in December, the garden need not look bare and cheerless, though it must necessarily be deficient in bright colours. First, there is always the rich green of the lawn, and that alone is a pleasant sight, and in many gardens there is a large stock of evergreens, both permanent, and used specially to fill in winter the beds which had in summer the gay bedders. In the generality of gardens these evergreens consist mostly of conifers and laurels, and neither of these do I consider very good for gardens of limited extent. I have no great love for conifers (with a very few exceptions), and in winter their stiff shapes and heavy colours are brought into a prominence that gives me little pleasure, though I must admit that they put on a wonderful beauty when heavily laden with snow. Nor do I much admire laurels as usually grown—that is, in thick masses kept trimmed and shorn, though an occasional one grown singly may be both useful and beautiful; but even so I would give the preference to the colchican and the round-leaved varieties over the common one. The Portugal laurel I do not grow at all, and I think it only fit for very large gardens, and even in those I have seldom seen one I could much admire. But of all evergreens I think there is none to compare with the holly, especially when allowed to grow freely and naturally; it is beautiful at all times, and in winter, especially when covered with its scarlet berries, it is a very precious ornament to brighten the garden.

But there are two classes of plants which I consider of especial value for the winter decoration of gardens—the variegated shrubs which do not shed their leaves, and hardy evergreen ferns. It is the fashion, especially among botanists, to despise variegated plants; they are said to be diseased, and to show their disease by their sickly appearance. This may be true, if the partial absence of chlorophyll is to be counted a disease, but it does not prevent their being very beautiful and very useful, and if vigour in growth is a sign of health, there are many instances in which the variegated specimens are hardier and more vigorous than the typical green forms. But I here claim for them a special value in the winter decoration of our gardens, and will name a few which I find most useful for this purpose. I have seen some of the variegated ivies covering a large extent of wall, and at a very small distance the wall seemed to be clothed with a rich creeper bearing an abundance of yellow or white flowers. All the variegated hollies are as useful; they brighten up a lawn in a wonderful way, and there are many to choose from, but I find that the variety with the large white blotches on the leaves produces the best effect. It is called, I believe, the milkmaid holly, but it has other names; and one peculiarity of it is its habit of bearing branches in which every leaf is of a pure ivory white; this, too, at a little distance looks like a bunch of white flowers, and if cut will keep its beauty in water all through the winter. I have also on a rock-work a large mass of the dwarf Japanese euonymus (*E. radicans variegata*), which I much prize. Not only does it lighten up the rock-work at all times, and especially in the winter, but it gives abundance of pretty sprays which are most useful both in the house and the church.

The second class of plants which I recommend for winter decorations are the evergreen hardy ferns. In most gardens the ferns are only grown in one fernery; I grow them everywhere, and, provided that the ground is not allowed to get too dry, they will flourish everywhere, even in the fullest exposure to sunshine. And as I walk round the garden in December their beauty is very striking, and I wonder that they are not more used to fill the summer beds with good winter foliage. Care must, of course, be taken with the selection when so used, but a good selection can easily be made. The athyriums die down with the first frost, and entirely disappear during the winter. The male ferns keep their foliage much longer, though they too get brown and withered before Christmas; but it is curious that the many crested and tasselled varieties of the male fern keep their fine foliage much longer than the typical plants, and I have known them keep their beauty all through the winter till the young fronds begin to grow in the spring. But the polystichums are absolutely evergreen, however severe the winter may be, and there are few ferns, whether British or exotic, that surpass them in beauty. It is the same with the hartstongues (*Scolopendria*) and the polypodies, and all their many varieties. Indeed, there are some of the polypodies which are, I think, at their best in winter, such as the Welsh polypody, and some others which come rather near it. I know of no foliage plant in winter that comes near to our Welsh polypody; in summer it is not so valuable, because it comes into leaf so very late, often not till nearly the end of July, but once the leaves are fully formed it will bear comparison with any. Though the typical polypody has a very wide geographical range, the Welsh polypody is almost confined to England and Wales, and is very rare in a wild state. It is, however, abundant in Teneriffe, and has been found wild in North America. There are also a few foreign exotic ferns, which are very hardy and evergreen, of which two very good ones are the Japanese *Cyrtomium*, and the North American *Polystichum munitum*, this last being, I think, the handsomest hardy fern all through the year that I know.

But though I think the garden must in December largely depend on evergreen trees, variegated shrubs, and evergreen ferns, yet there are still some good flowers to be gathered besides those I have already named. The *Clematis cirrhosa* will not flower every year, though I have often had it in good flower in December, but as it comes from Western France and the south of Spain, it requires more heat than our summers usually give it; when we have a hot summer and a mild November and December, then it will produce abundance of its pale buff flowers. But in almost every season I can pick flowers in December from the white variety of the dwarf heath of Southern Europe all through the winter.

I must say a few words about the laurustinus, which I mentioned last month, partly because it may almost be called the flowering shrub of December, but also because I overlooked some notes I had made on its literary history, which has one or two curious points. There can be little doubt that our plant is the *tinus* of Ovid, *Baccis coerula tinus*, and the *tinus* of Pliny, 'which differeth from all other laurels in the colour of the fruit, for it beareth blue berries,' and it is possible that the Latin word may be derived from the Doric τυννός (small); but when we are further told by

Miller (and others) that the word means the small laurel, and that the Doric word is the origin of our word 'tiny,' we may be allowed to doubt, for 'tiny' was an English word long before our ancestors began to make English words out of Greek. And I must also make good another omission in my last chapter. When noticing the curious fact of the growth of young and apparently tender foliage at a time of year when we should suppose the young foliage would be too weak to resist the frost, I omitted to mention what is, I think, the most remarkable as well as the most common example. The beautiful *Lilium candidum* is, perhaps, a native of Europe, but this is very doubtful, and its real native country is an open question, though Mr. Elwes, in his fine monograph on the lilies, rather inclines to Georgia. But it stands alone in this respect (and this may have some bearing on its native country)—that before the end of the autumn all its radical leaves are fully formed; and, as far as I know, no other lily ventures to show a leaf before the spring; and this is true, not only of the typical plant, but also of its varieties.

December is not the month for the full enjoyment of the garden; it is the month of pleasant memories, and it may be also of pleasant anticipations. By this I mean that a good gardener, as he looks round his trees and shrubs, and even his herbaceous plants, can form a fairly true estimate of his prospects for the coming year. In some cases he can do so almost to a certainty: in the rhododendrons, if he cannot say how many flowers he will have, he can count the trusses; and there are many others almost as much marked, as the spring-flowering magnolias. Or he can go among his fruit-trees, and tell almost to a certainty what his crop may be; among his pears, for instance (to take the commonest case), if he only knows the difference between fruit-buds and leaf-buds—it is very marked, and every gardener knows it—he can see to a certainty whether it is likely to be a good or bad year. Of course if his trees are not protected he will have to make a liberal discount for the robberies of bullfinches and other bud-loving birds, who in a hard winter will claim and take their full share; and he wil' have to make a still more liberal discount for spring frosts; but at any rate the flower-buds are there, and he can count them, and very pleasant and interesting work this is.

I am not fond of frost and snow, and the older we get the less we like it. But I have no doubt whatever that frost and snow have their uses, and that we should be all the worse without them. Many writers have taken the British weather as their theme, and shown how its endless changes and its harshness have done much to develop the character of Englishmen, of which an extreme instance may be taken in Kingsley's eulogy of and welcome to the north-east wind. But I am speaking only of the effects of frost and snow on English gardens, and I feel sure, though I may not be able to prove it, that much of the beauty of our English gardens comes from our English winters; for certainly our fickle seasons must have been the determining element in the character of our gardens, as, indeed, the seasons must be everywhere throughout the world. But however that may be, there can be no doubt that the interest of our gardens, and that which has made Great Britain a nation of gardeners, has been our fickle and comparatively cold climate. I have never seen tropical vegetation; my 'At last' has never come, and almost certainly will never be anything but an unfulfilled wish; but though I know that I should fully admire the glorious vegetation, I can fancy nothing less interesting from a gardening point of view. To have a garden where nature and the climate do everything, and man is called upon to do little more than scratch the ground and gather the flowers and fruit, might be very pleasant from one point of view, but it would take away all that to me constitutes the real interest of gardening, in its difficulties, and even its disappointments.

And so we will try and make the best we can of our English garden in December. 'The earth mourneth and languisheth,' but it is not all barren. Even Cowper, who, with his morbid melancholy, was at times full of cheerfulness, could say, speaking of winter—

> 'I love thee, all unlovely as thou seemest,
> And dreaded as thou art.'

But I go to a greater poet than Cowper. During Advent we always use the *Benedicite* in our Advent services; and as I read it in December I am forcibly struck with the way in which the writer speaks of winter. Whilst to almost every other 'work of the Lord' he gives but one verse or less of his grand hymn, to winter he gives no less than four—'O ye winter and summer,' 'O ye dews and frosts,' 'O ye frost and cold,' 'O ye ice and snow,' *'Benedicite Domino, laudate et superexaltate Eum in Saecula.'*

I have been asked by some, who seem to think that I grow many plants which are not usually seen in gardens of hardy plants, to say if I have any special rules for the successful cultivation of them. I know of no secrets in gardening, and I do not work or manage the garden on any hard-and-fast rules. If I have any rule, it is to leave my plants as much as possible to nature, and to let them grow in the ways which they choose for themselves. For this reason I dislike all tyings and nailings, all sticks, and everything that tends to cramp the free growth of the plants. Of course there is a limit to this freedom of growth; some plants must be tied for their own protection against wind, but such tying should be done as early as possible, for it is with plants as with ourselves, that the right way to train them in the way they should go is to commence with the 'child'. But for most plants I prefer cages. They are made, of different heights and diameters, of iron (technically called 'three-quarter round'), with three or four uprights and a few hoops. They are cheaply made, and last for ever; and I leave them in the ground all the winter, so that when the plants sprout in the spring they at once adapt themselves to the cage that surrounds them, and soon hide it with their foliage. It may seem a paradox to talk of a free natural growth and yet to recommend a constant use of the pruning-knife, but in practice the one is necessary to the other; and in nothing is the gardener's skill more shown than in the judicious use of the pruning-knife.

And when I am asked what qualities I consider most necessary in a gardener wishing to have and keep a good collection of plants, I name without any hesitation these three—patience, liberality, and a catalogue. Under patience I include perseverance and a prudent boldness, for the three go together. Without some boldness the gardener will make no experiments, and his garden will be no more than a copy of his neighbour's; but if he is bold enough to try experiments with his plants he will often meet with quite unexpected success, and a success which may be a real gain to others. I have always been fond of trying in the open ground plants which I have been told would only grow in the greenhouse, and I have been rewarded with many pleasant surprises, pleasant to others as well as myself. But, without speaking of myself, the great, almost national, advantage of boldness in making experiments with plants in fresh places is shown by the well-known examples of the tea, which in our own time was confined to China, but is now well grown in India and Ceylon; the cinchona, which so long was only to be found in Brazil forests, but now forms a staple article of commerce in India; the currants of commerce, which were always supposed to require the narrow Greek zone in which alone they could be grown without stones, but which are now grown successfully in Florida and California; where also is now grown the French plum, which only in the Garonne Valley could be made to produce the abundant juices that are so prized, contained in the thin but tough skin which enables the fruit to stand the high temperature of the kilns in which they are preserved. But such boldness is of little use without much patience and perseverance for success cannot be expected at the first trial; many trials in many different places must often be made before success is reached; and, of course, there will be many disappointments, but these need not be painful, and they have their uses, for in plant-growing, as in life, 'tribulation worketh patience, and patience experience.'

The second quality I name is liberality, which many years ago I was taught by an excellent gardener to be of the first importance in making and keeping a good collection. I have no sympathy with the feeling of satisfaction in being the sole possessor of a rare plant; I hold it to be true economy to divide and distribute as much as possible, for the selfish holder of the rarity will often find himself rightly punished by losing his one plant, and then not knowing where to look for it again.[1]

And the third requisite is a good catalogue; and I know from experience that I should have had great difficulty in getting my collection together if I had not always made it a practice to

[1]See p. 187.

catalogue my plants, and to keep the catalogue as accurate as possible. It forms at once the best letter of introduction to other gardens, showing what you want, and also what you may perhaps be able to give. But a good catalogue requires a careful naming of plants, and that, I think, a very pleasant part of gardening, though it sometimes requires much study to determine accurately the right name.[1] The study of plant names is by itself most interesting, and leads to much unexpected information. But for the good naming, some sort of label is necessary, and what is the best form of label is still an open question. I dislike wooden labels of all sorts—they are all too conspicuous, and for private gardens the label should be as little conspicuous as possible; in a public botanic garden they should be large, easily seen, and easily read. Here I have for many years used a cast-iron tally with a T-shaped head. This head is painted white, and when required for use has a thin coating of black quick-drying paint (Aspinall's paints do very well for the purpose), through which the name is written with any sharp-pointed instrument. The tally is almost invisible a few yards off, but the name can be read easily without taking it out of the ground.

I have now gone round the calendar, and my garden record is at an end. I have not attempted to give a complete list of all the flowers that can be gathered in each month; my object has rather been to show that there is no month in the year in which some, or indeed many, good flowers cannot be enjoyed. My own experience has been that a garden is a constant pleasure, and that the pleasure does not depend upon unbroken success. There will be many failures and frequent disappointments; there will be losses, sometimes of the flowers and fruits, and sometimes of the entire plants; there will be killing frosts, and long droughts, and unfruitful seasons; but the true gardener takes all these as necessary parts of his work—'minds quiet and contented take,' or may take, them all as necessary parts of the pleasure of his garden. That no season is altogether barren of pleasure, I hope I have been to some

[1] This study has now (1896) been made much easier by the completion of the *Index Kewensis*.

extent successful in showing; and when I hear people say, as some will say, that a garden is all very well in the bright months of a fine spring or summer, or even in the less bright months of autumn, but is altogether a dreariness in winter, or in bad seasons, I remember a song which was popular when I was young, which told of the pleasures of each season, and which ended—

'But know the best season to laugh and to sing
Is summer. is winter, is autumn, is spring.'

I cannot close my garden record better than by wishing to all my brother gardeners as much pleasure from their gardens as I can thankfully record to have received from mine.

PART TWO

CHAPTER XIII

SPRING FLOWERS

The earliest blossoms—Christmas Roses—Snowdrops—Crocus—Scilla—
Polyanthus—Anemone

To the true gardener—the man who loves his flowers—spring is perhaps the most enjoyable season of the year; to him, in very truth—

> 'Then comes in the sweet of the year,
> For the red blood reigns in the winter's pale.'

To him the reign of the red blood in the winter's pale is the season of happy hopes, the season in which he begins to look forward to triumphs which will now, he thinks, mostly certainly be his, the season in which he gladly allows hope to triumph over experience. And by 'spring' I mean not any fixed month, and certainly not any fixed day, on which, according to the almanack, 'spring commences', but I mean that time, month or day, in which he sees the resurrection of his much-loved plants, when every day shows some new growth, and when no day is like the last, but adds one or more treasures to be welcomed that have long been out of his sight; and so when each day brings a fresh pleasure, the earnest of, perhaps, fuller beauties to come, but scarcely of keener pleasures. At no other time of the year can the gardener have such a variety of hopes and expectations daily renewed and added to as he has in spring; and it must have been from some such feeling as this, that when Bacon drew out his ideal garden and stocked it with fair flowers of the whole year, his object was not to have perpetual summer, but perpetual spring—'My meaning is that you may have *ver perpetuum* as the place affords.'

'As the place affords' gives a very large margin to the time of the year at which the opening of spring may be placed. Fixing it by the time at which flowers first begin to show their new life, it may in many places be fixed even in January, for it must be an exceptionally cold January that cannot show some flowers. I may mention three that may be found in many gardens in January, and which are very interesting as giving a direct denial to the common idea that strongly scented flowers require bright sunshine to bring out their scents. They are the sweet-scented coltsfoot, with the scent of heliotrope, a native of the south of Europe, naturalised in some parts of England; the Japanese honeysuckle (*Lonicera fragrantissima*), with the scent of an orange-blossom; and the *Chimonanthus fragrans*, also Japanese, with a rich, heavy scent that is all its own.

These are welcome flowers of spring, but they lack brightness, and spring is full of bright flowers, the brightest of the year, bright in themselves, but most bright and most welcome by coming when they do. Let me name a few of them, confining myself to the earliest flowers of the year. There is the Christmas rose (*Helleborus niger*), a flower that would attract notice at any time of the year, but most welcome for coming, as it does, in the coldest and darkest days, and now so popular that we have in different parts Christmas-rose farms, from which the fine flowers of the purest white (otherwise unsaleable) are picked by tens of thousands in the fortnights before and after Christmas. But its popularity is no new fashion. It was probably introduced into England in the early part of the sixteenth century, and was highly prized. It was excellently described by Parkinson:—

'The flowers have the most beautiful aspect, and the time of his flowering most rare . . . It hath many fair green leaves rising from the root, each of them standing on a thick round fleshy greene stalke, divided into seven, eight, or nine parts or leaves, and each of them nicked or dented,. . . abiding all the winter, at which time the flowers rise up, . . . every one by itself, . . . consisting of fine broad white leaves, like unto a great white single rose, . . . with many pale yellow thrummes in the middle, standing about a green head.'

The plant is perfectly hardy, but capricious, growing and flowering without any difficulty in one garden, and refusing to grow at all in another; and there are many species and hybrids, all handsome plants, but not equal to the white one.[1] With the Christmas rose I may join the snowdrop, for they are often in

[1]See also p. 21.

flower together. Of all spring garden flowers none is such a teacher of hope. So it certainly was to Keble. To him it was not only the

> 'First-born of the year's delight,
> Pride of the dewy glade,'

but—

> 'I love thee, dear,' he said, 'because
> Thy shy averted smiles
> To fancy bode a joyous year,
> One of life's fairy isles.'

'The snowdrop,' says Forbes Watson, 'is a very star of hope in a season of wreck and decay, the one bright link between the perishing good of the past and the better which has not yet begun to follow.'

And almost, but not quite, as brave in fighting against difficulties is the whole tribe of crocus, especially the early golden crocus.[1] With the golden crocus will often come the 'pale primrose,' and it is very tempting to spend some time on this

> 'First-born child of Ver,
> Merry spring-time's harbinger,
> With her bells dim,'

from its many literary and other associations; but I must not do so, for it is a wild-flower, and I am now speaking only of cultivated garden flowers; and yet even so the primrose might claim a place, not only because it can be, and often is, used as an ornamental garden plant, but also because of its close brotherhood with the polyanthus, the most effective of all spring flowers when grown in masses, and one of the easiest to grow. One packet of seed will bring hundreds of plants, which will ornament the spring garden for many years. But, having gathered our pure white Christmas roses and our golden crocus, we may well join with them the gem-like blues of the two early squills—the *Scilla sibirica* and *Sc. bifolia*. These are small flowers, but not even the gentian sur-

---

[1] For a further account of snowdrops and crocuses, see p. 24ff.

passes them in richness of colour, and they are perfectly hardy; but within the last few years they have met with a formidable rival in the *Chionodoxa*, a beautiful bulbous plant discovered near Smyrna in 1842, but not introduced into England till 1877; and yet already, from its free flowering and abundance of seed, it has become in some gardens almost a weed, and when introduced into our woods, as is now being done, there is little doubt it will soon become completely naturalised, and be a companion and rival of our bluebells. The mass that was discovered by Mr. Maw on Nymph Dagh (4000 feet) was described by him as 'forming one of the most sumptuous displays of floral beauty he ever beheld, a mass of blue and white, resembling *Nemophila insignis* in colour, but more intense and brilliant'; and no one who knows the plant will doubt the correctness of his description.

But, even before the squills and the *Chionodoxa*, our spring gardens do not want blue flowers. We generally associate the iris with the early summer, but there are two that will flower in the midst of snow as beautiful as any of their summer brethren, and it is hard to say which of the two is most beautiful. They are the *I. stylosa*, of a very delicate blue, and sweet-scented, which comes from Algiers, Corfu, and the Morea, and of which there is a white variety of great beauty, looking like a white orchid; and the *I. reticulata*, a bulbous species, with a smaller flower of a rich deep violet colour, and sweet-scented, which comes from Asia Minor, Syria, and Persia. Both of these are perfectly hardy, and should be in every spring garden, and they come so early that the sight of them is really one of the first pleasant surprises of the year.

With one more colour I will conclude my account of the spring garden. I want a good scarlet, and I find it in the anemone—not our wood anemone, on which I now can say nothing, but the brilliant beauties of the south of France. Throughout the year we have no scarlet flower that will surpass the intense brilliancy of *A. fulgens*, especially the large Greek form, and it is as hardy as a bramble and as easy of increase. And as to abundance of flowers, I know of one vicarage garden in which this flower is a favourite, and is dotted about in many parts, and many hundreds of bright flowers are picked from the beginning of the year. It is one of the oldest inhabitants of English gardens. Whether it is the ἀνεμώνη of Bion that sprang from Aphrodite's tears, or the anemone of Pliny, is doubtful, but I like to think it is, and Theophrastus's description of it as flowering in the winter, and very shortly after its appearance aboveground, and that it is one of the ἐπιγειόφυλλα , favours this idea; and so does Pliny, who says, 'Some have a deeper and scarlet flower, others bear a purple flower, and there be again which are white. The leaves of these three be like unto parsley' (Philemon Holland's trans., 1601).

In this short sketch I have strictly confined myself to the *earliest* spring flowers; indeed, they might almost be ranked as winter flowers, or 'harbingers of spring.' Had I gone further, I should soon have found myself in that wealth of flowers which is seen in April and May, and includes the great families of tulips, hyacinths, violets, crown imperials, daffodils, even roses, and literally hundreds of other plants. And even within the narrow limits I have prescribed to myself, I have by no means exhausted the list of beauties that may be grown, but I have said enough to show that even snow and frost, and dark days and cold nights, will not prevent us, even in our much-abused climate, from having our gardens gay with flowers, which will not only delight us for their beauty, but will also teach us good lessons of hope and thankfulness. In January the days are dark and cloudy, and the trees are bare and leafless, but not always, and not for long:—

> 'Time will bring on summer,
> When briars shall have leaves as well as thorns,
> And be as sweet as sharp.'

CHAPTER XIV

SHRUBS

Good collections rare—Rhododendrons—Azaleas—Brooms and Gorses

DURING the last fortnight in April and the first fortnight in May there is something of a lull in the flowering plants. The pioneers of the year—the Christmas roses, the snowdrops, and crocuses—have quite passed away, and the daffodils, fritillaries, tulips, and hyacinths are fast following them, while the great army that will soon appear of pæonies, irises, roses, and lilies has not yet come into sight; and in gardens that trust to bedding-out plants there is nothing to be seen but bare earth in empty beds. Outside the garden the case is very different. In every wood and hedgerow that great outburst of life has begun in all its strength and exuberance which has given to May its many epithets—'the merry month of May,' 'all-beauteous May,' 'faire May, the fayrest mayd on ground,' and many such, all testifying to the joy that comes to us from the sight of the return to life of all the beauties of nature, with the promise that all things will again go forward in their normal course. Then only, and for a short time only, while the woods and hedgerows are covered with the tender greens which tell that the young leaves are bursting through their buds and are covering the trees with a beauty which as yet can scarcely be called full foliage, each tree stands out distinctly marked by its own peculiar shade of green, so that it is possible for a practised eye to distinguish between elms, oaks, and beeches, or between larches and Scotch firs. In June they will all be of an almost uniform green, dark, and even monotonous, and so they will remain till in autumn each tree will again assume its own peculiar brilliant hue, so that each can be readily distinguished from its fellow.

But in the flower-garden there is at that time no such variety. There are flowers to be found, and of much beauty, but they are not in abundance, and it is then that the gardener finds the great advantage of a good collection of shrubs. I wish, therefore, to recommend the growth of shrubs to a far larger extent than is usually seen, and I will give a short list of such as are useful in spring, and a few reasons why I strongly recommend them. But it is worth while to stop a little, and see what shrubs are as we have them now. The division of low-growing plants into shrubs and herbaceous plants is one easily recognised, but it is not a technical or scientific division. Shrubs occupy the debatable ground between herbaceous plants and trees, but the boundary-line on either side is not well defined, and is constantly being broken through. Many herbaceous plants might almost be called shrubs, and many shrubs (especially tender shrubs) die down every year, and so in our climate are herbaceous. Many shrubs also may attain the size of trees, and many trees are better treated as shrubs. But in speaking of shrubs I mean woody plants which do not die down in winter and seldom exceed 6 ft. or 8 ft. in height.

Of such shrubs we have now a very large number in cultivation in England, but it was not always so, and the cultivation of shrubs as we now grow them may almost be called a modern art. Down to the middle of the eighteenth century shrubs were chiefly used for making arbours and 'plashed alleys,' and were valued according as they were or were not useful to the topiarist. We read of 'groves,' but the bushes that composed them were very few; and even Bacon's heath, or wilderness, had only 'some thickets made only of sweetbriar and honeysuckle, with some wild vine amongst,' with 'mole-hills' set with wild thyme, etc., and 'heaps, with little bushes prickt upon their top.' Evelyn had a love for shrubs, and prided himself on having introduced the *Alaternus* from Languedoc, but his list of shrubs is a very poor one. The very name of shrub was almost a name of contempt, or at least it was chiefly used to mark the vegetation of a rough, wild country. Spenser's '*gloomy* glade was covered with boughs and shrubs.' In Caliban's country there was 'neither bush nor shrub to bear off any weather at all.' Etymologically, the word is the same as scrub; we still speak of a scrubby waste, and the word survives as a place-name in Wormwood Scrubs.

But in our day shrubberies ought not to be scrubberies, for our modern shrubs can no longer be spoken of as rough plants fit only for a wild common. Since the middle of the last century, many hundreds of hardy shrubs have been introduced from North and South America, Australia and New Zealand, China and Japan, and the Himalayas. Yet it is still a most unusual thing to see a good collection of shrubs except in gardens where the owner is something of a botanist. In the hundreds and thousands of new gardens that are made, the shrubs are left to the nurseryman, whose collection is limited to a few species which he supplies by the hundred to all alike. Yet it need not be so, and nothing gives so much character and charm to a garden, or so much breaks the monotony that makes so many modern gardens alike, as a variety of shrubs well chosen and well looked after. I will name a few, confining myself to those which are in beauty in the early months of the year, and excluding all that could be classed either as trees or climbers.

Where the soil is suitable there can be no difficulty in making the spring garden brilliant with the rhododendrons; but it is hopeless to attempt to grow them in soil in which there is the slightest trace of lime. But where lime is absent rhododendrons should be grown freely, both the European and American forms, in their many varieties, and, in the south of England, the grand Himalayan forms.

Where the rhododendron will grow, the azaleas and kalmias will also grow, and the three together will make a blaze of colour that is unsurpassed at any time of the year; but in the majority of gardens they must of necessity be absent; yet there are other shrubs that will brighten any garden. I must pass by our native gorse, in spite of its associations and beauty, to name its two foreign relations, the German and Spanish gorses, both very beautiful, and forming compact golden bushes which keep in flower for many weeks. With them I join their near allies the brooms; not our native broom, which, in spite of its rich golden colour, is too straggling and untidy except in shrubberies, but the small-flowered cytisus. Of this there are two sorts which are good ornaments for any lawn—the pure white *Cytisus albus* from Portugal, very pretty, though apt to grow in a thin and weak way, and the *Cytisus praecox*, a garden variety, which forms a close bush covered with lovely, pale lemon flowers, which last a long time, but cannot be picked on account of their heavy, unpleasant smell.

The barberries are all useful, both for their spring flowers and their autumnal tints, and they are easily grown, and keep in good shape. They are found in all quarters of the globe, and we have one in England which is interesting to the student of old English botany as being joined by the old writers with the box as an ornamental hedge plant, and bearing a name which has not changed (it is 'barbaryn tre' in the Promptorium), but which has never been explained. *Choisya ternata* is a beautiful shrub of the rue family, which, though known to botanists for more than sixty years, has only been introduced into England about twenty years. It is a rich evergreen, and in spring is crowded with its sweet-scented pure white flowers, and its buds are so like the buds of the orange that they are often used as substitutes. Though a Mexican plant, it is perfectly hardy, but likes to be sheltered from strong winds; and as it increases easily from cuttings, it ought soon to be in every garden. At present it is too much confined to 'the gardens of the curious.' And from Australia and New Zealand we have several of the daisy bushes, one of which, *Olearia Gunniana*, is a most desirable spring flowering shrub, the whole shrub being covered with white, daisy-like flowers, and perfumed with a fine aromatic scent.

I must not go further, though I should have liked to speak of the magnolias, spiræas, the Pyrus Japonica, the hardy orange (*Citrus trifoliata*, in flower at the beginning of May), the Californian bramble (*Rubus deliciosus*), the Daphnes, the Forsythias, and many others. Of roses, I could have picked specimens from the monthly China, but as yet roses are few. They will soon come in multitudes, and will require and deserve a chapter to themselves. What I have said of these few shrubs may serve as a guide-post to many others which I have not space to describe, and I wish to add a few words on the general advantages of growing shrubs to a much larger extent than is now done.

Shrubs, being perennial, make permanent masses on lawns, and so can be used as lasting objects in landscape gardening, in a way that herbaceous plants, however large, cannot. Being permanent, too, they improve every year in size, and generally in vigour; herbaceous plants reach the same height in each year that they reached the year previous, and no more; and shrubs do not in the autumn end in 'kecksies,' which require removal.

Shrubs, when fully grown, are near the eye—a matter of no little consequence when the time comes in which stooping is a weariness.

On rock-works, shrubs are indispensable, though most people are afraid of them; but a rock-work without shrubs looks bare and unnatural, and the great success of the large new rock-work at Kew may be largely attributed to the free use of shrubs.

I by no means wish to exclude the growth of herbaceous plants and Alpines—quite the contrary, and so I give as my last reason for the growth of shrubs that nothing is so useful as a protection for tender plants. It is too much the fashion to keep every plant in a border as separate as possible from its neighbour; but we have only to go to the nearest hedgerow to see how plants flourish by nestling into each other; and on the barest Alpine hillsides the plants love to get near the shelter of the low shrubs, and even grow so much among the roots as to appear almost parasitical. To dwell under the shadow of something better and stronger than one's self is as good for flowers as it is for man, and Spenser taught this truth in the pretty fable of the 'Oake and the Brere.' The whole tale is in the *Shepheard's Calendar* for 'Februarie,' and is much too long to quote at length; but it tells how 'a bragging brere' lived and flourished by 'a goodly oake,' how it took offence at the oak and got the master to cut it down, and then—

> 'Eftsoones winter gan to approache;
> The blustring Boreas did encroche,
> And beat upon the solitary Brere;
> For now no succour was seen him neere—
> Now 'gan hee repent his pride too late.
> For, naked left, and disconsolate,
> The byting frost nipt his stalke dead;
>
> Such was the end of this ambitious Brere
> For scorning Eld.'

I will merely add that no gardener will keep a collection of shrubs in good order unless he has a hard heart and a sharp knife, and uses them both with judgment.

CHAPTER XV

LILIES

Number of species—Difficulty of cultivation—White Lilies—Lilium auratum

IF spring is to the gardener the season of pleasant hopes and expectations, June is above all other months the month of hopes and expectations more or less realised. By the general observer the chief thing noticed is the full leafage of the month. So Spenser saw it:—

> 'After her came Jolly June, arrayed,
> All in greene leaves, as he a player were.'

And so in Coleridge's eyes it was 'the leafy month of June', and so it seems to be with nearly all the poets. But to the gardener it is the month of flowers; and if he were asked to distinguish the days of June from the days of other months, he would answer almost in the words of Aubrey de Vere, that they are the days in which

> 'The glorious sun's light . . . showers
> A thousand colours on a thousand flowers.'

But among the thousand flowers there would be two great families which would stand out supreme above all the rest, the lilies and the roses. And that is the unanimous verdict, not only of gardeners, but of all who in any degree love flowers. Their high popularity is shown in the way in which so many flowers which are neither roses nor lilies are so called. In Miller's *Dictionary of English Names of Plants* there are one hundred and eighty-eight plants named which are called lilies, of which only seventy are true lilies (*Lilium*); the rest are such plants as lily of the valley, water-lily, St. Bernard's lily, Mariposa lily, Belladonna lily, etc. In the same way, but not to the same extent, flowers are called roses which are no relations to the genus rose, as the Christmas rose, guelder rose, rock rose, rose campion, rose of Sharon, etc. To be called a rose or a lily does not mean that the bearers of the name are either roses or lilies, but it gives them a diploma for grace and beauty.

Their popularity is further shown by the great number of books that have been written on the two families. The strictly botanical books about them reach a large number, while the books that sing their praises incidentally must be almost innumerable. In all gardening books they necessarily fill a large space, and in all gardens with the slightest pretence to completeness both must be seen in abundance. And just as Horace thought them necessary in a feast—

'Neu desint epulis rosae,
Neu vivax apium neu breve lilium'—

so in every well-ordered garden there must be *lilia mixta rosis*.

My subject, then, is the lilies and roses of June, and the lilies first—a very hackneyed subject, some will think, and certainly it is, if by that is meant that already much has been written on it, but there is no finality in gardening or in gardening literature. More than two hundred years ago Evelyn laughed at those who gave 'the glorious title of compleat and accomplished gardeners to what they have published, as if there were nothing wanting or further to be expected from the field, and that Nature had been quite emptied of all her fertile store', and he prophesied the great increase that must be always looked for in our knowledge of the products of nature. This is so remarkably the case with lilies, that it is worth while to look back and compare our present abundance of these beautiful flowers with the very scanty supply which called forth the loving admiration of our forefathers. Theophrastus only mentions one lily, and Dioscorides two; Pliny describes three, but it is very doubtful whether they are all true lilies. In the Middle Ages the lily must have been a rare plant, for it is said that no representation of it in old illuminations is found earlier than the fifteenth century, though it is certainly represented in paintings before that time. Gerard, in 1597, described twelve species, which his editor Johnson about forty years later increased to twenty-one. Parkinson describes fourteen, but some of them are varieties. Bauhin about the same time arranged all the then known sorts of lilies under twenty-eight species, which Linnæus reduced to eight. Our latest authority, Mr. Elwes (in his splendid monograph of the family), describes forty-seven good species, besides varieties.

Of these forty-seven species none are truly native in Great Britain, though one (*L. martagon*) is considered to be naturalised in Surrey; but the geographical range of the whole family is very extensive, so much so, that M. de Cannart D'Hamale says: 'La nature a voulu orner de ces belles fleurs toutes les contrées du globe, à l'exception peut-être de l'Australie.' They are not, however, found in Africa, or anywhere within the tropics. Eight are found in Europe, thirteen in America, and the remainder in Asia, chiefly in Japan and the Himalayas.

The cultivation of some of the lilies is difficult, and nearly all of them are capricious, and refuse to follow any fixed rules of cultivation. But they are probably all hardy in the south of England, and with very few exceptions they are hardy anywhere, so that it is rather surprising that they are not more grown than they are. Yet it is a most unusual thing to see a good collection of lilies, and even in gardens which aim at variety the lilies are usually represented by no more than three or four species. Every one grows roses, but lilies, which can be as easily and as cheaply obtained, are often found best in the cottage gardens. This is especially the case with the common white lily. There is no more beautiful lily, and none to which are attached so many pretty legends and stories, or with so many associations, historical and poetical. Its native country is uncertain, but it is undoubtedly this lily that has been longest in cultivation in Europe. Virgil's lilies were *Candida* and *Grandia*, and it was from very early times the flower of the Madonna. He would be a well-read man who could bring together all that has been written on this universal favourite, and it would fill a large volume. Yet, though so common and such a favourite, it will not grow everywhere. In many gardens it lives a few years and then disappears. In my own garden it will only survive if planted almost under a tree; and I have a recollection of the envy with which I once looked at a row of cottages in a village under the Wiltshire Downs, where, in the little gardens in front of the cottages, this lily seemed to grow like a weed. I believe there are two secrets, or rather two things, to be remembered in the cultivation of lilies; one is that most of the lilies are wood-plants, and so, though they require sunlight, and free circulation of air, they certainly do better in partial shade; and it has been found that the grand golden lilies (*L. auratum*) nowhere do better than when planted amongst rhododendrons, which shade the roots, and do not prevent the flowers from rising into full sunlight. The other rule is not to keep the roots long out of the ground, and, indeed, to keep them, if possible, entirely undisturbed. This may be one reason why they often do so well in cottage gardens—they are let alone; and this was the rule among the old Dutch gardeners, as laid down by Laurembergius in 1632, 'Si eximendi sint e terra liliorum bulbi, protenus aut paucis diebus interpositis reponantur.'

In my garden I find that the easiest to grow are *Martagon* and its varieties, *Croceum*, *Testaceum*, *Pomponium*, *Pyrenaicum*, and *Californicum*; but if I had to do with another garden, I should not be surprised to find that my experience would be very different.

In one respect roses bear the palm over lilies. Nearly all roses (except some of the modern hybrids) are sweet-scented, while a very few lilies are so; most of them are scentless, and some are quite offensive; and the lily does not bear picking as the rose does. A rose-bush in full flower can spare many flowers and yet not lose its beauty; you cannot pick single flowers from a spike of lilies without spoiling its symmetry, and it is almost a cruelty to cut down the spikes entirely, for they can only be utilised in tall vases.

In another respect, too, lilies are curiously different from roses. I know of only two species which produce double flowers, the white and the pompone, and these doubles are both ugly. But the roses seem to have a natural tendency to vary with double flowers; they can be counted by hundreds, and are increasing every year, and they are all beautiful flowers.

Though I know by experience the difficulty of growing many of the lilies, and though I recognise that in some points they fall short of the popularity of the rose, yet I would advise all to try as many species as they can procure. They will not succeed with all, but success with any will give a character to any garden. I am not very successful with them, yet no flowers that I grow give more

pleasure to my friends and myself, or add so much to the gaiety of
the garden. I think that Englishmen never have for the lily the
same affection that they have for the rose, their feeling for it is
more of admiration than affection; but even so, they are surely
worth growing in as large quantities as our gardens will allow.
They are easily obtained; success with them is a great delight, and
failure with a few will not involve much loss of labour or money;
and so I say again, *manibus date lilia plenis*.

I must not enter on the poetry of the lily—the field is far too
large. It may safely be said that scarcely one of our English poets
has failed to speak, and to speak lovingly, of the flower. From
Chaucer downwards to our own day our poets tell of its beauty
and grace, and with all of them, I believe, the lily alluded to is the
white lily. To take one instance only, and very shortly.
Shakespeare not only expressly says that the lily is white, 'white as
a lily,' 'the lily's white,' 'the lily pale,' 'the lily white,' but he uses
'lily' as an adjective equivalent to 'white,' *e.g.* 'the lily-tincture,'
'lily lips,' 'lily hands,' 'lily livered,' 'lily fingers.'

CHAPTER XVI

ROSES

Double Roses—Wild Roses—Eglantine—Homes of the Roses—Their age—
Austrian Brier

'IN May and June come roses of all kinds, except the musk, which comes later,' says Bacon; and though I so far follow his lead as to place the rose among the chief glories of the garden in June, and though it is in June that they are seen in the fullest abundance and beauty, yet it is one of the great charms of the rose that they brighten our gardens for so many months of the year. We may almost say that, weather permitting, a good garden is never entirely without roses in flower. I have picked good flowers from the monthly China roses in January, and in 1888 I picked a good bunch of fairy roses on Christmas Eve. I know of no other flower that can come near the rose in this respect; the daisy possibly comes the nearest. This may perhaps be gathered during nine months of the year, but very seldom in November, December, and January. And this must be one of the reasons (independently of the beauty and scent) why the rose is so dear to us, and is so closely interwoven with English country life. It is not only that it is the national emblem, and has been so from very early times, for other nations have national floral emblems, which do not enter into their home-life as the rose does with us; nor is it because it is surrounded with so many historical associations—the red rose of Lancaster, the white rose of York, the Tudor rose, the musk roses, and the eglantine of Shakespeare and Milton;—but it is, I think, that from its easy cultivation, especially in our climate, it is found in every garden, and can be grown in full beauty in the great gardens of the rich, but in equal beauty in the small garden of the poorest cottager. It is the favourite everywhere; in the child's garden, and in the garden of the florist, who watches and nurses it for exhibition—pruned or unpruned, highly cultivated or neglected, it is always beautiful and always prized.

For the florist there is scarcely more than one type of rose, the fine double hybrids which have been produced from the two species, *Rosa Gallica* and *Rosa Indica*. But I do not propose to speak of them, not because I do not admire them and value them, but their beauties and all their points of excellence can be found fully described in the pages of Rivers and the Dean of Rochester. But there are three double roses that are such special favourites with me for different reasons that I must say some little about them. One is the old cabbage rose, a rose so much neglected that a few years ago it could only be found in a few old gardens, and in cottage gardens. Yet it is a rose of a wonderful scent which no other rose has, and its historical interest is very great. Not only is it the red rose of England and the 'provincial rose' of Hamlet, but it is probably the oldest cultivated rose we have, so old that its native country is unknown. One of its names with us is the hundred-leafed rose, and under that name it was recorded by Theophrastus and Pliny (ἔνια εἶναί φασιν ἅ και καλοῦσιν ἐκατοντάφυλλα— Theoph., *Centifolium vocant*, Plin.). It is the parent of the moss roses and of the pompone, or *de Meaux*, and of many others now gone out of cultivation. A second favourite double, or semi-double, rose is the York and Lancaster, of which there are two kinds; one a very old rose, in which the petals are sometimes white and sometimes pink, and sometimes white and pink in the same flower. This is without doubt the 'roses damasked, red and white,' the rose 'nor red nor white had stolen of both' of Shakespeare, and it is the *R. versicolor* of the old botanical writers. In the other sort the petals are a rich crimson, flaked with white; it is a very handsome rose, comparatively modern, and is the *Rosa Mundi* of the *Botanical Magazine*, t. 1794.[1] The third double rose I wish to notice is one commonly called the yellow cabbage. It has, however, no relationship to the cabbage rose, and its origin is unknown, but it was a great favourite with the old rose-growers, and is now again slowly coming into cultivation. It was first described by Clusius, who noticed it among some coloured paper models of gardens sent to him from Constantinople. Lindley describes the flowers as 'very large, of an exquisitely delicate,

[1] I may refer to a paper in the *Gardeners' Magazine* for Aug. 12th, 1893, in which I put together all that I could find of the history of the York and Lancaster rose.

transparent, yellow colour';[1] and as I write with the flower before me, just picked, I can answer for the truth of the description. The weak point is that the flowers seldom fully open; they probably require a hotter sun than they usually get here, both before and at the time of flowering; but even in this unopened state it was a favourite with the Dutch painters, especially Van Huysum. There is a fine picture by him (belonging to Lord Ashburton), in which this rose in its half-opened state forms part of the foreground, and which is well known to collectors of mezzotints as forming one of the fine engravings by Earlom in 1778 from the Houghton pictures.

But I leave these few doubles to speak of some of the wild species of roses which, though little grown except in botanical collections, are full of beauty and interest. There are about fifty species of the genus *Rosa*, found in all quarters of the world, but only in the north temperate zone. Plenty of roses are grown in Australia, New Zealand, and the Cape, but they have been introduced by colonists. Of course I cannot speak of all these fifty species, I can but select a few. In Great Britain there are (according to Sir J. Hooker) seven good species with many varieties, of which at least two are garden favourites. One is the Burnet rose, a very pretty little rose as found on our seashores, and the parent of all our Scotch roses; and the other is the sweet-brier. This is certainly the eglantine of Spenser, Shakespeare, Milton, and all the old writers, and though not common as a wild plant, it can be found in many parts of England, especially in the chalk districts. It has perhaps the most delicate perfume of all roses, and of all British plants, and it has the faculty, especially after rain, which all sweet-scented flowers have not, of giving out its scent without being picked or handled. It is one of 'the flowers and plants that do best perfume the air,' 'yield the sweetest smell in the air,' a fact which Pliny also noticed: 'The eglantine will cast a sweet and pleasant smell, although it reach not farre off' (Holland's trans.). The plant seems to have a special fascination for great lawyers. Bacon, in the sixteenth century, names it five times among his favourite plants, and it seems to be

[1]Lindley called it *R. sulphurea plena*. Its correct name is *R. hemisphaerica*.

equally acceptable to a great judge of our own day. Many may have been surprised, and perhaps a little amused, to find that at the Rose Conference in 1889, Lord Penzance read an excellent paper, not on the woes of 'the aggrieved parishioner,' but on the delights and capabilities of the sweet-brier.

From Europe we get the white rose, which has been so long naturalised in England that it is sometimes admitted into the English flora. It is the white rose of York, and if we could believe the elder Pliny's derivation of Albion, *ob rosas albas quibus abundat*, it would be our oldest cultivated rose. In its semi-double state it is a favourite cottage rose, and deservedly so, for the flowers are a very pure white, and the bush, though large, is never untidy, and requires little or no management. We also get from the south of Europe the alpine rose, and its pretty red-leaved variety. This is distinguished from nearly all roses by being entirely destitute of thorns, except in the young shoots; and it is one of the parents of the Borsault roses, once very popular, which show their parentage by being also for the most part thornless. *Rosa Gallica* is found in many parts of Europe; as a single rose it is not often seen, but it has given rise, not only to innumerable garden hybrids, but also to some natural hybrids, of which the old damask rose, much beloved of our forefathers, is now said to be one.

From Asia we got many of our most beautiful roses. China, Japan, and the Himalayas have each in turn sent us their treasures. From China we have the Macartney rose, a grand rose in its single state, with pure white petals, golden stamens, and shining leaves, but spoilt when double. From China also we have the delightful Banksias, generally the earliest rose that flowers, and with very sweet-scented double white flowers, but also with double yellow flowers that are almost scentless. The single Banksia is almost unknown in England, and one of my chief remembered delights in my garden was the first sight of this rarity in flower in 1890. The flowers were a pretty pale yellow, slightly scented.[1] Both the Macartney and the Banksia rose require a wall, but the China roses (also from China, though called *R. Indica*) are as hardy as a bramble. I am very fond of this rose, in all its

[1] See pp. 40, 53–4

varieties; it is, as I said before, almost ever-flowering, and it has been the parent of many of the finest hybrid roses. From Japan comes the beautiful Ramanas rose, *R. rugosa*, a rose unsurpassed where it will grow well, as it does in my garden, with splendid thick foliage, and large handsome fruit, which are said to make a good preserve.

But it is from N. India and the Himalayas that some of our best species of roses come. This is probably the native home of the musk rose, as it is of the *Rosa multiflora*, a charming rose, rightly so named, for though the flowers individually are small, the trusses of flowers are wonderful: I have counted on one truss (meaning by that the part projecting beyond the leaves) over six hundred flowers. This species also is the parent of many hybrids, but in all of them one curious resemblance to the parent is always seen in the finely serrated stipules; each stipule is like the finest saw. I can only mention one rose from Persia, though we get more than one from there, and that is the *R. berberifolia*, a rose that differs from all other roses in having a single leaf instead of the usual three, five, seven, or more divisions, and which from its earliest introduction has been the despair of gardeners. It is now at last successfully grown at Kew and in the Isle of Wight, but how long the success will last is doubtful. It is to Asia that botanists are now looking for new species. It is well known that there are some in Japan which are as yet not grown in England, and in 1888 a grand new rose was discovered in Upper Burmah by General Collett, which promises to be a king of roses; it is a pure white single rose, 6 ins. across the petals, and has been well named *R. gigantea*.

The roses of Africa are only found in the north and are the same as the South European species, and I must not stay long with the American species. There are not many, but there are two at least that are worth a place in the garden. The *R. lucida* forms a close bush with deep-green shining leaves, bright rose flowers, and bright red fruit. Though in America it is almost a marsh plant, it will grow anywhere, and the double form produces the prettiest buds for button-holes that I know. The *R. Carolina* is not a showy rose, but it flowers late in the autumn, and so is valuable; it has also some interesting botanical curiosities, on which I cannot now dwell.

This is not much more than a very slight sketch of the wild roses—not only of the wild roses in general, but of those few which I have named. I wish to show that there is beauty and interest in multitudes of roses which would find no place in a rose show, and with this object I will mention two or three points which recommend them. They are all very easy of cultivation. 'The first quality of the rose', said St. Francis de Sales, 'is that it grows without artificial aid, and has hardly any need of being cultivated, as you see roses in the fields growing up without any cultivation,' and on this he founds a good lesson. This is especially true of the wild species: they are better let alone, they do not require, and indeed they dislike, the knife. Another point of excellence in them is that, although (with the exception of the China roses) they are in flower but a short time, they are followed by fruit of great variety and much beauty. No one who has not seen a collection of these roses can have any idea of the variety and beauty; they are of all colours, from black and green to brilliant red, and of all sizes and shapes.

The literature of the rose, both botanical and otherwise, would fill a good space in any library, and I must not attempt to say more than that a very good selection of the poetry of the rose was published in 'E. V. B.'s' pretty little book, *Ros Rosarum*. It was, however, only a selection, and did not pretend to be more. But on one literary point I must say a few words. Favourite as the rose is, and always has been, in England, it has no English name, and seems never to have had one. I fancy that its old English name was brier, a true English word, and that it was not till after the tenth century that the Latin *rosa* was applied to the flower, retaining the 'brier' for the bush. In the Epinal glossary (eighth century) there is no rose, but there is 'brear,' and rose first appears in Archbishop Ælfric's glossary in the eleventh century. Then gradually the 'brier' was dropped, and both bush and flower were rose, but they were still distinguished in Shakespeare's time, *e.g.*—

> 'Of colour like the red rose on triumphant brier.'
> 'From off this brier pluck a white rose with me.'

Roses grow to a great age. I have a Banksia on my own house that is certainly seventy years old, and may be older, and I have no doubt there are many roses in England very much older; and if we can believe the legend, there is a rose at Hildesheim, in Lower Saxony, that is more than a thousand years old, the cathedral being built for it and over it in A.D. 815.

Roses have a slight economic and medical value, but their commercial value is very small, except to the nurseryman. The rosewood of commerce does not come from the rose-tree, but from Brazilian and West Indian trees of very different botanical families; and the brier-wood pipes, so dear to smokers, are not made from the sweet-brier, but from the white heath (bruyère) of the south of Europe.

Walking round my garden with a special eye to the roses, I see that in what I have written above I have omitted many things that deserve notice; I therefore continue the subject, beginning with a rose which stands alone in colour, not only among roses, but almost among all flowers; this is the Austrian brier, and its whole history is curious. No one knows its origin; it is supposed to be a variety of the single yellow rose (*R. lutea*), itself a very scarce rose in a wild state, though said to have been found wild in Germany, France, and Italy. The earliest notice I have been able to find of it is in Parkinson's *Theatrum Botanicum*, 1640, where it is described as 'the single dwarfe red rose of Austria.' The colour is quite peculiar: a deep crimson inside, and yellow, almost golden, outside, and if seen against the light, the yellow will affect the crimson or the crimson the yellow, according as it is looked at from the inside or the outside. I know of only one plant with the same remarkable combination of colour in the petals, the *Potentilla Macnabiana*, of the same family as the Austrian brier (the *Rosaceae*). There is, however, a flower in which the calix is a dull crimson and the corolla a bright yellow, and, rather curiously, that too is connected with Austria,—I mean the *Abutilon vexillarium*, which obtained the name of *Vexillarium* because the colours are those of the Austrian banner. In another respect the Austrian brier is different from all other roses. We naturally connect roses with a sweet scent:—

'The rose looks fair, but fairer we it deem
For that sweet odour that doth in it live.'

Yet many of the modern hybrids are quite scentless, and the Austrian brier has actually an offensive scent, so that it was called by the old writers '*Rosa foetida*,' '*Rosa graveolens simplex flore extus rubro intus luteo*,' while a modern writer says, 'Ray says that the flowers smell like honey; to me they smell more like bugs.' I can only say for myself that the evil smell is much exaggerated; it exists, but is very slight, and must be sought for. But it is not a popular rose, because it is difficult of cultivation, or rather capricious. The Dean of Rochester, the great master in rose-growing, has said that he cannot grow it. I grow it, but not as well as I should wish, while in a neighbour's garden it grows like a weed, sending up suckers in every direction; and in a neighbouring village the rectory-house had once a grand specimen trained to an east wall, and in the flowering season (unfortunately a short one) the plant seen in full sun with many flowers open was really a gorgeous sight. And that reminds me to say that this is a very good way of growing the sweet-brier. I do not know why it should be so, but the sweet-brier is seldom grown near the house, probably because it will grow anywhere, and house-walls are valuable for more tender plants. Bacon recommended it as 'very delightful to set under a parlour or lower chamber window', and so I saw it once at Tintern—not under a window only, but trained to the top of the house (a two-storied one), and surrounding both upper and lower windows. Th effect was very charming, and I was told that when once established it was very easily kept in order.

It would be inexcusable to omit all mention of the musk rose among the single roses. Its native home is the north of Africa, but it must have spread into Europe in very early times, and it was brought into England from Italy. So we are told by Hakluyt: 'The artichowe was brought in time of King Henry the Eight, and in later times was procured out of Italy the Muske Rose plant.' As soon as it came it established itself as a chief favourite, and became the typical emblem of floral beauty. Shakespeare makes it the special rose of Queen Titania. Milton names it among the choicest flowers to be strewn on Lycidas' hearse, though perhaps he only uses the name in a general way—his knowledge of flowers was very limited,—for in *Comus* he makes the shepherd speak of 'musk roses of the vale,' as if they were some wild English roses. This high estimate of the musk rose—

> 'The sweetest flower wild nature yields,
> A fresh-blown musk rose'—

is a little surprising to us, for it is not a very attractive rose, and is now very seldom seen, having been supplanted by its near relation, *R. Brunonii*, from Nepal, probably only a geographical variety of the old musk rose, but a very handsome rose, especially when allowed to wander among and over bushes, for it does not like pruning or training. To these roses I will merely add, and strongly recommend, a very modern rose, Paul's single white perpetual. I do not know its history, but it is a very beautiful single rose, with clusters of large pure white flowers, which last in flower a long time, and I know of few better roses for a pillar.

The more I study roses the more I feel that we northerners have good reason to be proud of them, and to be thankful for them, and Englishmen especially have good reason for taking the flower as, above all others, the flower of England. When Mr. Wallace returned from the Malayan Archipelago, fresh from all the beauties of tropical vegetation, he astonished many English readers by asserting that English wild-flowers gave a beauty of colour to English landscape which no tropical flowers give to their native countries. And so it is with the rose. In our climate we cannot grow many of the beautiful shrubs which are so prized in the gardens of Southern Europe, and our meadows and hillsides cannot show the abundance and variety of flowers that are found in Swiss meadows and hillsides, but we have the rose, and with us it grows both wild and cultivated with a freedom and beauty that are nowhere surpassed. William Browne, in 1613, sang its praises:—

> 'A rose, as fair as ever seen i' the North,
> Grew in a little garden all alone;
> A sweeter flower did nature ne'er put forth,
> Nor fairer garden yet was never known.'

And I am sure that there can be no more beautiful sight in wild nature than an old English hedgerow when the untrimmed dog-roses are in full flower, and no garden can show more beauties in June and July than an English garden well stored with roses of all kinds.

But the wild roses give us a lesson in growing roses in the garden. I do not like roses in pots or budded on high standards. I know their uses when so grown, and if I grew roses for exhibition I should perforce grow them in one of those ways, but roses require to be free and unrestrained to show their full beauty, and roses grown as lasting ornaments in the garden can scarcely be too much left to themselves. Some require walls, and so must be trained, but they will grow beautifully against a tree, or over bushes. The *Rosa Brunonii* is described as growing in India, with 'its white flowers appearing on the largest trees, and filling the air with a powerful scent for long distances', and so it is grown in perfection at Kew, rambling over bushes; and I once had on my lawn a very large old box-bush, of little beauty either in shape or colour, but allowed to remain because from the centre grew an old Ayrshire rose, which in summer clothed the box-tree with wonderful beauty. When the rose died I cut the box down. And even the finest hybrid roses rejoice in this treatment, and they are so easily propagated that there is no difficulty in getting a good stock of plants, which may be treated in many different ways. Long cuttings from this year's ripened wood planted deep in the open ground in November will often produce plants that will flower the following year.

I said that there was no real English name for the rose, and it is remarkable that it is the same in Eastern countries—they also have no native name for it. So Sir Dietrich Brandis stated at the Rose Conference:—

'The rose has no true Sanscrit name, which pointed to the fact that roses which had been cultivated by the Mohammedans for centuries previously were first introduced by them into India after their conquest of that country. In India, in days long before the Mohammedan Conquest, there were gardens, and in Sanscrit songs flowers were praised, but the rose was not amongst them.'

As there must always have been abundance of wild roses in India, the absence of a name is very remarkable.

And there is one point in the literature of the rose that should not be passed by, and that is the complete change of sentiment with which the French and English writers have looked on the rose as compared with the Greek and Roman writers. By the Greeks and Romans the rose was always connected with scenes of revelry and licentiousness (a few passages on the fleeting character of the flower notwithstanding). It was dedicated to Venus, Bacchus, and Cupid, and in the phrase *sub rosâ* we still perpetuate its connection with banquets and revelry. I believe it is much the same with the Eastern poets, but I have too little acquaintance with them to speak positively. Madame de Genlis counted among the triumphs of Christianity the conversion of the rose, 'profanée par la mythologie et par le culte paiën', to the uses of the Church. This may be a little far-fetched, but it is the fact that the feelings connected with the rose by French and English writers are entirely different, except in the few cases where the writers have copied from the heathen or Eastern poets. By French writers the rose is made to teach the decay of beauty, especially of female beauty. By English writers the lessons have a tone of sadness, and often almost of sternness. They cannot, and do not try to, escape the obvious lessons of decay of all that is lovely and pleasant on earth, but it is curious that it is the thorns of the rose that seem most to have caught their attention, and from them they draw two very different lessons. They love to point to the rose and its thorns as showing the treacherous character of all earthly pleasures; but they love also to point to the thorns as forming only a part of the rose, and a necessary part, to perfect and protect the rich flower; and so, while on one side the lesson is that no pleasure is without pain, *rosa inter spinas*, so, on the other side, there is the brighter lesson, that troubles lead to joy—*per spinas rosa*—*per tribulos caelum*.

CHAPTER XVII

CLIMBING PLANTS

Clematis—Vines—Honeysuckle—Smilax—Growth of climbing plants

CLIMBING shrubs, when properly used, are great helps in a mixed garden, and I often wonder that they are not more used, but they really are very seldom seen, except when trained to walls. But, in speaking of climbing plants, I do not mean such as are trained and nailed to walls, but such as are allowed to climb more or less by their own unassisted powers over arches, poles, or some other support; and I mean to speak of hardy perennial climbers only, and so exclude annual and tender plants, though there are many such that are very beautiful and useful.

First and chief among such climbers comes the clematis. The name originally meant merely a branch of a vine, but afterwards was extended as a name for almost all climbing plants. Pliny included several such under the name; Gerard says that clematis is 'a certain genericke name to all woody winding plants, having certaine affinitie because of the spreading branching and semblance of the vine'; and Parkinson has a chapter headed, 'Clematis, Clamberers or Creepers,' and the chapter begins with the periwinkle and ends with the passion-flower. Of the true clematis we have one beautiful representative in the traveller's joy (*C. vitalba*), 'decking and adorning waies and hedges, where people travel, and thereupon I have named it traveller's joy,' says Gerard; and his name has clung to it, though it has not supplanted the older name of 'ladies' bower,' or 'virgin's bower,' the last name having been given to it in honour of Queen Elizabeth, though it has been claimed as one of the flowers dedicated to the Virgin Mary, and so the flower of August 15, the festival of the Assumption:—

'When Mary left us here below
The Virgin's bower begins to blow.'

In the late autumn it changes its name to 'old man's beard,' from the beautiful silky heads of seed which often cover the banks and hedges for many yards in length with wonderful grace and beauty, and which, if picked in good time, will keep in beauty all the winter. This lovely climber is found in almost all parts of Europe, from Holland to the south, and its popularity is shown by its having no less than two hundred different names in different European languages. In Great Britain it is found in almost every part of the south, and, though it seems to like the chalk best, it will grow anywhere, but it is not found truly wild in Scotland or Ireland. I must not, however, dwell longer on it, for it is a wild plant, and I have to speak of garden plants. I know of no family more useful in the garden of hardy plants than the climbing, shrubby forms of the clematis, for there are some herbaceous species of which I cannot speak now. But of the climbing sorts there can be had plants of all colours—pure white, deep blue, pale yellow, purple, and so up to the brilliant scarlet of the *C. coccinea* from Texas. And they can be had at all seasons, for I have often gathered the trusses of the lovely white *C. Montana* from the Himalayas in March, while the South European *C. cirrhosa* will give its pale buff flowers in midwinter if the season is not severe. And in all of them the beauty is not confined to the flowers; the foliage of many is most delicate, and the seeds almost as beautiful as those of our own wild traveller's joy.

There are two very good climbers of a much more limited range than the clematis, the *Periploca* and *Aristolochia*, both of which will very rapidly cover anything to which they are attached. The *Periploca Graeca*, which covers the hedges in many parts of Greece, is one of the most rapid and one of our oldest garden climbers. It was grown and admired by Gerard and Parkinson, and is sometimes seen in old gardens, but it is not common. It is, however, well worth growing; it has bright green leaves, and an abundance of trusses of black and green flowers, followed by a curious seed-vessel, formed of two pods joined at the two ends, and open in the centre, and full of pretty silky threads; but I have never seen the fruit except on plants against walls. The whole plant is full of a white, milky, poisonous juice, and it has the reputation of keeping flies away from any room against which it is planted; this I do not fully believe, though it is certain that this juice, if exuding from a broken spray, would act like birdlime on any insect unfortunate enough to touch it. The *Aristolochia sipho* is a better known climber, very rapid in its growth, with large, heart-shaped leaves, and curious flowers, 'Dutchman's pipes,' which are fatal to numberless small insects, the internal construction being exactly similar to an eel-trap. It is a native of America, and was brought to England about the middle of the last century, and grows well in and near towns. There are many species, but this is the hardiest.

Vines make beautiful creepers, and though, when grown away from a wall, they produce few or no grapes, they are all worth growing for the beauty of the foliage—beautiful in the various shapes of the leaves, and most beautiful in their autumnal colours. Some take this colour very early in the season, especially the claret vine, which often takes its rich claret colour before the end of June, and keeps it till the frost strips the tree. I grow several vines simply for the beauty of their leaves, and I especially recommend the old parsley-leaf vine, of very delicate foliage, and often ripening its clusters of small, black, and sweet grapes, and the sweet-scented vine of America. I need not say how much of historical and legendary interest attaches to the vine, which makes it doubly attractive, but on which I must not even enter.

But of all hardy climbers I suppose the most universal favourite is the honeysuckle; and it is a truer climber than any I have mentioned. The clematis and the vine can be made to climb easily, but they require some help; the honeysuckle will cling to anything near it, and clasp it tightly, whence its old name of woodbinde, a name, however, which it shares with other wild climbers, as the ivy, clematis, etc. But the name is very appropriate; for every boy knows, and every wood-labourer likes to cut, the sticks (generally hazels) round which the honeysuckle has grown, 'oftentimes winding it selfe so straight and hard about that it leaveth his print upon those things so wrapped' (Gerard). Our British species may well find a place in any garden, and for sweetness it will scarcely have a rival; but there are others of great beauty, such as the scarlet trumpet honeysuckle from South America, and the Dutch honeysuckle, and there is one from

China, *L. fragrantissima*, which can be grown as a climber, but will also form a bush, and which has the great merit of producing its orange-scented, though small, flowers in January. Before leaving the honeysuckle it may be worth mentioning that the name is one of our oldest English names—it is found in the *Epinal Glossary* at the beginning of the eighth century—but has not yet been satisfactorily explained.

With a few more climbers from different parts of the world I will conclude my list, though it might be much extended, and I must describe them very shortly. The Canadian moonseed (*Menispernum Canadense*) is an excellent climber, with long wreaths of very pretty foliage. The flowers are greenish, and of no beauty, and I have never seen the seed, which gives the name to the plant, as it is dioecious, and I have only the male plant, but it is described as bearing berries like frosted grapes, with a moon-shaped stone inside. The *Akebia quinata* is another rapid climber, with beautiful, five-leaved foliage and almost black flowers, very sweet-scented—these are not often produced, however, unless the plant is grown against a wall; but it is quite hardy, and was one of Fortune's discoveries in China.

I have reserved to the last two plants of extreme beauty, but very seldom seen. One is the smilax or sarsaparilla, which I think in all its forms is the most beautiful climber I know. The flowers are small and inconspicuous, and I never saw the berries produced in England, but the foliage of all the species cannot be surpassed, growing, as it does, in long wreaths, bearing leaves of exquisite shape and bright green colour. The South European *S. aspera* is well known, and in the Riviera the sprays with the bright berries form the most useful Christmas decoration; but there are other species from China, Japan, America, and Australia, of greater beauty and equally hardy. And with the smilax I join the asparagus—not our common edible sort, but some of the many little-known, but most beautiful kinds, of which some can be grown as hardy plants. For the most part, gardeners know only the edible species and two or three grown as greenhouse basket-plants; but Mr. Baker's list (our latest and best authority) gives ninety-seven distinct species, of which some may rank among our best hardy climbers. I grow three such, and have no doubt there are others equally good and hardy. The three I grow are *A. Verticillata*, which here is deciduous, but by the end of May it produces grand shoots, 14 ft. or 15 ft. in length, clothed from top to bottom with lovely sprays of deep-green feathery foliage, which last all the summer till cut down by frost. Another is *A. acutifolius*, not so beautiful and not so hardy, as it seldom does well away from a wall, but evergreen; and the third is A. medeo-loides (*Medeola asparagoides*), from the Cape of Good Hope, a universal favourite, generally grown in greenhouses, but perfectly hardy.

As to the way of growing these creepers, it must be left to the taste of each gardener. They may be grown on arches of iron or chain, or on arcades built after the fashion of an Italian pergola. Either of these ways will give pleasant shade, and when properly treated become good additions to any garden. But I prefer poles of oak or fir, roughly trimmed, because I think the plants prefer them. They may be placed singly in the centre of flower-beds, or by the sides of paths, or two or three together, with different plants to each, allowed to intermingle. These rapidly get covered, and form excellent ornaments to a garden, taking up very little room.

It is impossible to speak of climbing plants without a short reference to Darwin's researches into their nature, as shown first in his paper on the *Movements and Habits of Climbing Plants*, published in 1865, and then in his larger work on the *Power of Movement in Plants*, published in 1880, a work which, though not perhaps so popular or so well known as some of his other works, yet shows, I think, almost more than any other, his untiring patience in observation, and his wonderful power of drawing out great principles from the most minute and (to others) insignificant properties of organic life.

I must note, also, an interesting point connected with the philology of climbing plants. In America all climbing plants are called vines; and it sounds strange to us to see the name given to such different things as the vine, the Wistaria, the clematis, the ivy, the honeysuckle, the scarlet runner, etc. But the name is not a modern Americanism, and I am inclined to think (though I cannot prove it for certain) that the early settlers brought it from

England.[1] The writers of the sixteenth and seventeenth centuries called many plants vines; and Halliwell, in his *Dictionary of Archaic Words*, says that vine is the name for 'any trailing plant bearing fruit', but he gives no authority for the statement. We have, however, a record of it in the old plant-names—white vine, wild vine, wood vine, blood vine, hedge vine, Isle of Wight vine, etc.

I will conclude by going back again to our own beautiful wild climber, the traveller's joy, that I may quote Bishop Mant's address to the flower:—

> 'The traveller's joy!
> Most beauteous when its flowers assume
> Their autumn form of feathery plume—
> The traveller's joy! name well bestowed
> On that wild plant, which by the road
> Of Southern England, to adorn
> Fails not the hedge of prickly thorn,
> Or, wilding rose-bush apt to creep
> O'er the dry limestone's craggy steep;
> There still a gay companion near
> To the wayfaring traveller.'

[1] 'Vine' is so used in 2 Kings iv. 39: 'found a wild vine, and gathered thereof wild gourds.'

CHAPTER XVIII

GARDEN WALLS

Cheddar Pinks—Cacti—Alpine plants—Stonecrops—Emblems from wall-plants

AN old garden wall is a very precious possession to a gardener. If he finds himself placed in a new garden surrounding a new house he may by much expenditure of labour and money soon get a well-filled garden, but if ever he goes into the garden of a friend who owns an old garden, surrounded or bounded by an old wall, he feels that his own garden wants something which only time can give him. For an old wall is, or may be, very useful to gardeners; I do not mean for training trees—a new wall will do for that as well, or better—but for planting on it many things which there find their most congenial home. Nature teaches us the lesson by the way she clothes, and clothes rapidly, old ruins; but I do not wish to say anything of this natural clothing of old walls, except that it is well worth noting how many plants seem to prefer these old walls even to well-tilled ground near them. I never saw the beautiful small white periwinkle (an uncommon plant anywhere, and even doubtfully native) so luxuriant as I once saw it on the walls of Tintern Abbey. As it grew there I could easily fancy that it was an escape from, and perhaps the last remnant of, the old Abbey garden, and for the first time I realised how well adapted the plant was to form the 'garlands of Pervenke set on his heaed' that Chaucer and other old writers sing of; but the plant is no longer there, having been destroyed by a succession of admiring and greedy visitors. And many of us recollect with pleasure the South European *Senecio squalidus* at Oxford. It probably escaped from the botanic garden, and now clothes, not only the grand old coped wall of the gardens (a wall that is almost unequalled as a garden wall), but also the walls of the park of Magdalen, and even grows freely on the stringcourses of Magdalen tower.

Any one who possesses an old wall will find plenty of plants that will grow there as well, and in many cases even better, than on the borders; and it seems to make little difference of what material the wall is made. I have seen granite walls almost as well covered as those made of a softer stone, and slate walls soon get covered; but the best walls for the growth of plants are those made of oolite or sandstone. In many parts of the country, especially in the sandstone districts, the wall is finished with a thin layer of stones slightly projecting, and upon this projection are placed, vertically, stones of various thickness and height, which thus in time form 'pockets' of old mortar mixed with much vegetable matter arising from dead leaves and weeds, which make happy homes for many good plants.

Chief among such plants I place the Cheddar pink. In its native home on the Cheddar cliffs it grows chiefly in small tufts on projecting ledges of the cliff, and brought into the garden it is not an easy plant to grow in the open border, but it can be easily grown if its root uninjured (as it seldom is when bought at Cheddar) is inserted under the coping-stone of a wall. In that position it will flower freely, and increase by growing downwards; and such plants I have on the wall of my garden, which have probably been there for more than sixty years, and live and flower without any attention or protection; and in a garden near Bath I have seen a plant which, originally placed on the top of an old freestone wall, now hangs down in a beautiful mat, more than five feet in length, and three feet across. And I believe the same treatment is good for all the tribe of pinks. We learn this from our own wild carnation (*Dianthus caryophyllus*), the parent of all our carnations, and the gillyflower of our ancestors; this is only found wild on our old castles, and never, I believe, in hedges or fields. To me it has always been a plant of great interest, because knowing it to be an alien, and having seen it in great abundance on William the Conqueror's own Castle of Falaise, I like to think that it was introduced either by him or some of his followers; though its seeds or some plants may have been imported with the Caen stone. But I mention it now because this gives an excellent hint for growing carnations. As usually grown, they are sadly stiff, and a bed of carnations shows almost as many sticks as flowers. But in Switzerland they are grown (especially the crimson cloves) in the window-boxes of the chalets, and are allowed to hang down, and so grown they are very beautiful; and exactly the same treatment may be given to all carnations. They may be placed either on the top of a wall, or in the chinks, and will there grow naturally with excellent effect.

The hardy cacti will grow well in holes of old walls, and generally with greater vigour than when grown in the open ground without shelter. But it is well to give them some protection from snow, for snow will rot them, and the protection can easily be given by a slate or piece of glass, or by inserting them under the shelter of the coping-stones. Their chief enemy then will be the snails, who manage to get at their succulent leaves in spite of the poisonous spines with which they are protected. And, indeed, this is the chief objection to old walls; they are the favourite haunts of many enemies to the garden. In course of time the mortar decays, and the wall is full of holes; where these are at all large they are apt to get filled with colonies of snails. If the holes are in the lower part of the wall, mice will take possession of them, and I have found slow-worms even in the higher holes, but these do no harm. But it is to the insect world that all the holes in an old wall become most attractive, their warmth and dryness exactly suiting them. Alphonse Karr, in his *Tour round my Garden* (in spite of its discursiveness, still one of the pleasantest of gardening books), has a special chapter on an 'Old Wall'; but, while he gives a few lines of praise to its vegetable beauties—'in the crevices of its top extends an absolute crown of yellow wallflowers and ferns, and at its foot vegetate pellitory and nettles in all their beautiful green'— yet his chief delight is in the animal life of the wall—the lizards, caterpillars, and spiders.

But it is for the growth of alpines that the old wall is especially useful. In many gardens it is found very difficult to grow the beautiful cobweb stonecrops (*Sempervivum arachnoideum*). But the late Mr. Wilson Saunders, a most successful cultivator of rare and difficult plants, used to grow it well on a bare stone without any soil, and in such a position I have grown it several times, till it gradually gets destroyed by the damp atmosphere. The first time I saw it growing wild was on a narrow ledge of the old bridge at Hospenthal near Andermatt, and there it was so feebly attached to the stone that the slightest touch dislodged it. I have no doubt it would grow on any wall, but if put high upon the wall its wonderful cobwebs would be invisible; yet it might be worth growing even there if it would produce its flowers, which are of a rich crimson colour, but it is a shy bloomer out of doors in most parts of England.[1] Many of the saxifrages are very difficult to grow out of doors, but two of the most difficult and most beautiful, *S. florulenta* from the Maritime Alps, and *S. longifolia* from the Pyrenees, are now grown successfully and easily at Kew by inserting them in the horizontal crevices of a wall-like rock-work. Another alpine that can be treated in the same way is the edelweiss. Not many years ago it was considered almost impossible to grow this plant away from its alpine fastnesses; now it is found to grow easily if raised from seed, and at the gardens at Trinity College, Dublin, it is grown as a wall-plant, in projecting hollow brackets specially used for it and other plants like it. Another alpine which is very apt to 'miff off' if grown in the open border is the *Erinus alpinus*, yet I once saw the fine old brick coped wall which bounds the garden of Denton Hall, in Buckinghamshire, completely covered with this pretty alpine in full flower, and since that I have seen it on other walls, but not in such abundance as at Denton. I have no doubt that many of the alpine primulas and androsaces would grow on old walls, but I have not tried them; and, indeed, I think that most plants which can stand drought and delight in bright sunshine would be worth trying, but it would be of little use to try bulbs, though some tuberous plants, such as the dwarf irises, would certainly grow in such positions. I say nothing of wallflowers, snapdragons, and foxgloves, for they are native plants which will sow themselves; but seeds of the better sorts are worth sowing, and I will only name one more flower which should be planted on every wall where it does not grow naturally, the wall toad-flax, *Linaria cymbalaria*. This is not a true native, and is said to have been brought from Italy, though found wild as far north as Holland, but it is completely naturalised in many parts of the United Kingdom. It is one of the most

[1]See paper on Wall-gardening at M. Boissiers in *Gard. Chron.*, June 1890, p. 791, and September, p. 265.

graceful wall-creepers that I know, and with me it grows naturally; but if it did not I should certainly plant it. The flowers are
usually a pretty purple, but I have found it with pure white flowers,
and there is a variegated form; all are lovely ornaments for any
wall.

King Solomon knew 'the diversities of plants and the virtues of
roots,' and he wrote of 'the hyssop that springeth out of the wall,'
as well as of 'the cedar tree that is in Lebanon,' and since his time
many writers have followed his example, and have written of
wall-plants, not only or chiefly from the botanical point of view,
but for the obvious lessons which such plants teach. I have seen in
some old book of emblems (but I cannot now recall the name) the
emblem of a flowering plant springing from a wall, with the motto,
'Rebus in arduis servare mentem,' and this has been the keynote
with all such writers—the springing forth of healthy life, and the
growth of beauty in places where, naturally, we should least
expect to meet with them. I must find room for a few such. In the
middle of the seventeenth century T. Bailey, Sub-Dean of Wells,
was imprisoned in Newgate. While there he published (in 1650) a
queer romance, 'A History which is partly True, partly Roman-
tick, morally Divine,' which he called *Herba Parietis; or, the Wall
Flower as it Grew out of the Stone Chamber belonging to the Metropolitan Prison of London, called Newgate*. The title page is an interesting
engraving of old Newgate, and from the hood mouldings of the
upper windows on each side of the gateway there spring wallflowers in full flower. The idea is the somewhat conceited idea of
a beautiful work coming from a dreary place. The other instances
which I will quote are pleasanter, because not so conceited. In *The
Antiquary*, Sir Walter Scott makes Edie Ochiltree, when hiding in
the ruins of St. Ruth, moralise pleasantly on 'the wallflowers and
siccan shrubs as grow on thae ruined wa's,' and to draw from
them 'a parable to teach us not to slight them that are in the
darkness of sin and tribulation, since God sends odours to refresh
the mirkest hour, and flowers and pleasant bushes to clothe the
ruined buildings (ch. xxi.). But of all references to flowers on the
old walls I think there is none more touching than in Cardinal
Newman's account of his departure from Oxford in 1846. I must
give it in full:—

'I took leave of my first college, Trinity, which was so dear to me. . . . Trinity had never been unkind to me. There used to be much snapdragon growing on the walls, opposite my freshman's rooms there, and I had for years taken it as the emblem of my own perpetual residence, even unto death, in my University. On the morning of the 23rd I left the observatory. I have never seen Oxford since, excepting its spires as they are seen from the railway.'—*Apologia*, p. 369.[1]

It would be unpardonable in speaking of the literature of wallflowers to leave unsaid Tennyson's well-known lines, with which I may conclude my paper:—

> 'Flower in the crannied wall,
> I pluck you out of the crannies;
> Hold you here, root and all, in my hand,
> Little flower—but if I could understand
> What you are, root and all, and all in all,
> I should know what God and man is.'

[1]See also a Poem on the Snapdragon in *Verses on Various Occasions*, p. 17, by J. H. Newman, 1827.

CHAPTER XIX

AUTUMN LEAVES

Maples—Salisburia—Tulip-trees—Medlars—Creepers—Value
of autumn tints

PLANT-LIFE is full of mysteries, and none greater than the changing and falling leaves in the autumn. We know many facts about it, and we can mark many of the changes which come before and after, but there still remains a vast amount of mystery which we cannot solve. I cannot even attempt to write on the general physiology of these great changes, but I can say something of the great pleasure that every gardener can (and, as I think, should) take in the wonderful beauties of autumnal foliage. American writers tell us that we in England are not qualified to speak of the beauty of trees in autumn, that we must go to their great forests if we want to see the fulness of beauty that autumn can show. They tell us that, while in England 'a soft pale yellow is all one sees in the way of tints along the borders of the autumn woods,' in America there are 'six weeks of Indian summer all gold by day, and, when the moon comes, all silver by night;' and 'when the maples have burst out into colour, showing like great bonfires on the hills, there is indeed a feast for the eye':—[1]

> 'Arrayed in its robes of russet and scarlet and yellow,
> Bright with the sheen of the dew, each glittering tree of the forest
> Flashed like the plane-tree the Persian adorned with mantles
> and jewels.'—LONGFELLOW.

From all accounts, this is not an exaggerated description, and to American eyes our woods in autumn must seem tame in colour; but they have a beauty of their own, and—

> 'The pale descending year is pleasing still.'—THOMPSON.

And though I wish to speak chiefly of the foliage in the gardens, I

[1]Burroughs.

cannot altogether pass by the beauties of trees in our woods and hedgerows. One of the first trees to put on autumnal colours and to drop its leaves is the horse-chestnut; in some seasons the leaves take the colour of old gold, and when they fall the curious horse-shoe mark at the junction of the leaf with the branch is so distinct that it is not surprising some should think the name of the tree is derived from that, with which, however, it has no connection. The elms and beeches soon follow the horse-chestnut, and colour the woods and hedgerows with large masses of pale gold and the richest russet red. The hedges themselves do not show much colour, unless they are old; then they are coloured with the spindle-tree, the black berries of the privet, and especially the maple. Some old hedges are now composed entirely of maple, and are very beautiful in their autumnal tints; yet it is quite certain that the maple was never planted as a hedge-plant, and it has often been a puzzle to me how it could have established itself so as to have strangled all the original plants. I think I have found the explanation in Evelyn's *Sylva*, a book now, I believe, very little read, but in Sir Walter Scott's opinion it should be 'still the manual of British planters, and the author's life, manners, and principles as illustrated in his memoirs ought equally to be the manual of English gentlemen' (*Kenilworth*). He says that the maple 'is observed to be of noxious influence to subnascent plants of other kinds, by reason of a clammy dew which it sheds upon them.' This clammy dew gives the maple a great advantage in the struggle for existence, and we get the benefit of it in the autumnal beauties of our old hedges filled with maple.

But I must leave the woods and hedgerows for the garden. The late Miss Marianne North had seen trees in all parts of the world, and with an artist's eye, and she often told me that she knew nothing in foliage more beautiful than the *Salisburia* in its autumnal tints. I know of few better trees for a lawn; in its early stages it grows more slowly, but when fully established it grows rapidly, and becomes a tree always of a good shape, and with light, graceful foliage. Botanically it is a most interesting tree. Though closely allied to the yew, it is as unlike a yew as possible, and the leaves have a really wonderful resemblance to the maidenhair fern. It comes from China and Japan, and often bears its Japanese name, ginkgo, but it is more commonly known as the maidenhair-tree. I have never seen the flowers or fruit, and they are seldom produced in England;[1] and it has the further interest that, though only introduced a little over a hundred years, it is an old inhabitant of England, both the leaves and fruit being found in some of the carboniferous strata. In some years the autumn foliage is of a rich golden colour; and the leaves are so slightly attached to the branches that even in midsummer a high wind or a sharp shower will almost strip the tree, and bring down a 'rustling shower of yet untimely leaves' (Thompson).

Almost as beautiful in the autumn is the tulip-tree, and it has the advantage of holding its leaves for a long time after they are well coloured; and both for flowers and foliage (also of a very peculiar shape) it is a noble tree for a lawn, but care should be taken not to have a flower-border near it, for its roots spread far, are very near the surface, and are very exhaustive, and will soon starve any plants with which they come in contact.

Parrottia Persica is a beautiful shrub, or small tree, to grow on the lawn or in the shrubbery for its autumnal effects only. It is still a rare tree, though it has been introduced from the north of Persia about fifty years, and in spring and summer it is not an attractive tree, but in the late autumn each leaf becomes a splendid mixture of rich brown and crimson and yellow, while the base of the leaf very often remains a deep green, so showing a combination of colour that exists in no other shrub. It is perfectly hardy, but if grown against a wall the leaves remain longer on the trees, and the colours are rather richer. It is named after Professor Parrot, who made the first ascent of Mount Ararat in 1829, and not in allusion to the colours.

I think no lawn should be without a medlar-tree. It is a tree that always throws itself into a good shape, and in the south of England is worth growing for its fine white flowers; but even where it does not flower it becomes a fine mass of golden yellow in the autumn, and the leaves will remain on the tree till frost comes.

Another shrub well worth growing for autumn is the flowering

---

[1] In a few instances the fruit has been produced in England by grafting the two sexes on the same tree. By this means fruit has been produced at Worcester.

currant (*Ribes sanguineum*), of which the autumn foliage is as beautiful as the spring flowers.

The Virginian creepers are too prominent on many houses to need more than a passing notice. The different sumachs are very fine objects in autumn, and I name them to recommend one of great beauty, the low-growing *Rhus glabra laciniata*, and to warn all gardeners against another, the North American poison oak, *R. venenata*, which is splendid in autumn, but which is a most dangerous plant to have in a garden. I must also add that some herbaceous plants have very richly coloured autumn foliage, as the broad-leaved *Statices*, some of the meadow rues (*Thalictrum*), and especially the autumn cyclamen (*C. hederaefolum*), which, though not of a brilliant colour, must be reckoned among the best of autumn foliage plants, for the leaves do not show themselves till the autumn, and they remain in wonderful beauty till the spring.

I often think that botanists do not take sufficient notice of the colouring of the leaves in autumn; so far as I know they do not notice it at all, I mean in the scientific description of the plants. It is now a canon in scientific botany that the entire structure of a plant has reference only to the forming and perfecting of the seed, and when that work is done, the different offices of roots, stems, branches, leaves, and flowers are at an end. Mr. Ruskin will not even go so far as that, but limits all the useful life of a plant to the formation of beautiful flowers. Yet surely the tinting and the fall of the leaves must have their uses in the life of a plant, and the autumnal tints of our trees and shrubs are so distinct, one from another, that many of them are more easily distinguished in autumn than in summer. And we may remark that many trees which can show no beauty in flowers, show a beauty in autumn surpassing the flowers of many flowering shrubs, of which the elm and the beech are good examples; and many of our exotic trees which have become naturalised never bear seed (the common elm never ripens seed in England), and yet we cannot say that their life has been in vain. And I like to think that the tree has not done its full task till it has delighted us with the brilliancy of its autumn leaves; in other words, I think that the energy of the plant has been all along directed to the perfection of its life in autumn, quite as much as to its life in spring and summer, and that the autumn tint

is as specific a character as the colour of the flowers. One effect of
the fall of the leaf is very manifest: if our trees kept their leaves all
the winter they would probably all be weeping trees. Few people
realise the great weight of leaves. I have on my lawn a mulberry-
tree with a flower-border very near. To give light to the border,
the tree was trimmed one winter, so that every bough was at least
five feet from the grass. But when the leaves came the boughs
bent down to less than fifteen inches from the ground; when the
leaves are gone the boughs rise again; but if they remained, the
tree would very soon assume the character of a weeping tree. And
what has occurred and been noticed with that tree must be more
or less true of all.

It is a great puzzle why the tints in some years are much brighter
than in others. In some way it must depend on the amount of rain
and sunshine, and probably it depends chiefly on the amount of
sunshine, for the bright summer of the Jubilee year ended in a
richly coloured autumn; and I suppose that the same atmospheric
conditions which are needful for the ripening and colouring of
our fruits are also needful to the ripening and colouring of our
leaves; and as the botanist carefully notes the forms and colours of
the ripe fruits, it seems to me that he leaves part of his task
unfinished when he takes no notice of the forms and colours of
the ripe leaves.

Poets and moralisers in all ages have said so much of the fall of
the leaf in autumn that a large volume might easily be filled with
this one subject. But it would be a very sad volume, for few seem
to have been able to escape from the obvious lessons of decay and
death. A few there have been who have taken brighter views of the
season; as Forbes Watson noted:—

'The last leaves shiver from the trees, and the last ripe fruit drops pattering to
the earth, and these relics do not tell us of a dreary time, and the very sadness of
autumn is swallowed up in the sense of its more than earthly loveliness.'

But most of the writers seem to have taken the one text only,
'We all do fade as a leaf,' and to have written accordingly. And yet
the coloured and the falling leaf is not a sign of death, it is rather a
sign of the fulness of life and vigour. It is only when a branch is
dead that its leaves are dull and wrinkled, and cling to the branch

all the winter, but the full-coloured and falling leaf shows that it has left behind it a plump, vigorous bud, into which its life has passed, and which holds in itself a colony of leaves, and flowers, and fruit. Every gardener knows that a cutting which keeps its withered leaves will come to nothing, but that if they fall it shows that there is full life behind. I wish more of our writers could have seen how much of good allegory might be drawn from this view of the fall of the leaf instead of the more dreary view that all is over. Yet I know of none that have so looked on it. Cowper came rather near it in the 'Winter's Walk at Noon,' but he missed it; and the nearest approach to it that I know is to be found in Homer's well-known lines, οἵη περ φύλλων, etc., which I will give in the old translation of Chapman:—

> 'Like the race of leaves
> The race of man is, . . . the wind in autumne strowes
> The earth with old leaves, then the spring the woods with new endowes.'

CHAPTER XX

PALMS AND BAMBOOS

Origin of the names—Different species—Hardiness of Bamboos—Biblical
references

I JOIN these two families together, for though they have no
botanical relationship, they are always associated together when
writers speak of tropical scenery, and they are the only plants in
our gardens which in any way recall the tropics to those who have
seen anything of tropical countries. But I wish to speak chiefly of
those which can be called hardy; they constitute a very small
portion of the two families, but they are beautiful objects in any
garden; they are easily obtained, and when once established are
most easy of cultivation; yet it is a most unusual thing to see a good
collection of them.

It is only in recent years that either palms or bamboos have had
a place in English gardens, and their exotic character and modern
introduction are well shown in their names. Many exotic plants
have been so long established that they have good old English
names, but there is nothing English either in palm or bamboo, yet
there is an interesting history in both the names. It is not easy to
see why the Romans should not have taken the Greek name
φοίνιξ for the palm; yet for some reason they did not, except to a
very small extent, but they took a part of it. They rejected the
name of the fruit δακτύλοι (whence our 'dates'), but instead of
the fingers they took the Greek name for the whole hand
(παλάμη), and so called the tree *palma*, and from that we took
our 'palm.' The name bamboo is even more curious. The native
name for the plant, or the name by which it was first known in
Europe, seems to have been 'mambou,' and so it is called by
Gerard and Parkinson, and that was easily changed into bamboo.
But that was not all; the native name was Latinised into *bambusa* (I
believe by Linnæus), and is one of the very few native names of
exotic plants that have been so used; tobacco (Latinised into
tabacum) and potato (Latinised into *batatas*) are other instances,

but these are both given to distinguish a species and not a genus.

It is not easy to say when our ancestors first became acquainted with the palm as a living plant. It was described by Theophrastus, Aristotle, and Pliny, and the plant described by all of them was the date palm; for though Pliny says that there were many sorts of palms, it is evident from his descriptions that he was only speaking of varieties of the date palm. In English literature the word occurs in all the old vocabularies, but simply as a translation. Neckham described it, but probably had never seen it; but from the frequent allusions to it in the Bible, the early Eastern travellers took full notice of it and described it minutely. It seems very certain that neither Shakespeare nor Milton had seen the living tree, for Shakespeare only speaks of it as a proverbial and legendary tree, and Milton's only epithet for it (in three places) is 'the branching palme,' a most unfitting epithet, for it is the characteristic of almost all palms, except the doom palm, to be unbranched, and he speaks of a 'palmy hilloc' in connection with lawns, and downs, and groves, thornless roses, and grapes. Both Parkinson and Gerard describe the trees, but do not say that they had seen them, though they both tried, and not successfully, to rear young plants from the fruits, which, under the name of finger apples, had been imported into England from very early times. When the living plant was first grown in England I cannot discover; but Miller grew the date palm in 1731, and in 1768 five species are recorded to be growing at Kew.

It would be too long a task to enter into all the scientific botany of the palms, but two points may be shortly noticed, one connected with the geography of the plant, and the other with the history of scientific botany. The geography of the plant is curious. Its chief home is in the tropics, but it stretches into the borders of the northern and southern temperate zones. It is found in Asia, Africa, and America, Australia and New Zealand; but in Europe the only species is the *Chamærops humilis*, which grows near Nice, the extreme northern limit of the family, while the extreme southern limit is marked by a single member in the southern island of New Zealand. But the curious thing about the geographical distribution of the family is that of the vast number of species and varieties (there are said to be nearly 1200 species of palms, and in North Africa alone nearly 40 varieties of the date palm), each species (with very few exceptions) occupies a distinct and limited area, within which only it is found. It is as if each county in England had a separate rose or bramble, found nowhere else but in that particular county.

In the history of scientific botany the palm holds a remarkable position. The plants are for the most part (though not always) diœcious, the male and female flowers being borne on different plants. Linnæus is generally credited with having discovered the different sexes of plants; but Theophrastus, Aristotle, and Pliny were all taught by the palm that there were male and female flowers, and that the one could not produce fruit without the other.[1] They do not seem, however, to have carried their observations in this direction much further than the palm, though Pliny says—

'All learned men who are deeply studied in the secrets of nature be of opinion and doe teach us, that in all trees and plants, nay, rather in all things that proceed out of the earth, even in the very hearbs, there are both sexes. But there is no tree whatsoever in which this distinction of male and female appeareth more than in palme trees.'—xiii. 4, *Holland's Translation.*

And he proceeds to describe both the natural and artificial fertilisation of the flowers. But the idea did not take root. Parkinson was well acquainted with Pliny's works, and in describing the palm, he says—

'The ancient writers have set down many things of dates, that there is male and female, and that they both beare fruite, so that they be within the sight one of the other, or else they will not beare, but I pray you account this among the rest of their fables.'—*Theat. Bot.,* 1547.

In 1662, Johnston, in the *Dendrographia* (ii. 5), said, 'Palma fructifera vel est mas vel foemina,' and described the process of fertilisation, and evidently believed in it. Yet still the idea was not

[1] The bisexual character of the palm and the artificial fertilisation were certainly known to the ancient Assyrians and Babylonians. See *Flora of the Assyrian Monuments,* by Dr. Bonavia, p. 74; and *The Dawn of Civilisation,* by Professor Maspero, p. 555.

accepted by botanists till Linnæus fixed it, and found that what was true of the palm was true of all other living plants.

I said that there were 1200 different species of palms; but of this large number only three or four can be at all considered hardy in England. The hardiest is without doubt the Chusan palm, *Trachycarpus Fortunei*, introduced a little over forty years ago by Fortune. It was not at first tried as a hardy plant, but the experiment was soon made (I believe first at Osborne), and it was found to be perfectly hardy; and when it has been established eight or ten years it will commence flowering, and will generally flower every year. It is a very beautiful and graceful plant. All it asks for is protection from wind, and it should be planted where it can have some screen from the prevailing winds, but it does not mind frost or snow. In my own garden it grows about ten feet high, and forms splendid leaves. The only other species that can be considered hardy is *Chamærops humilis*, but it will not compare with *C. Fortunei*, and is not so hardy. *Jubæa spectabilis*, from Chili, will grow in Cornwall, and *Pritchardia filifera* has survived some winters in very favoured places. *Brahea nitida* is said to be the hardiest palm in the Riviera, and *Cocos australis* at Genoa, but I have not heard of their being grown out of doors in England, and *Erythæa armata* (*Brahea Roezelii*), from the Rocky Mountains, may perhaps prove hardy.

The cultivation of the hardy palms is perfectly easy. The Arabs say that they require to have their feet in cold water and their head in a furnace. This combination we cannot give them, nor is it necessary; they only require to be planted in good soil, to be protected from wind, and not disturbed, and when once established they give no further trouble, and they give a continual delight to the grower.

It is easy to pass from palms to bamboos, for though they are not botanically related, yet they seem almost to pass into each other at some points:—

'Their relationship will probably be thought rather distant by those who, from want of other materials, compare the meadow-grasses of the temperate zone with the cocoa-nut trees of the tropics; but it will become more apparent when the huge bamboo, as the representative of the grasses, is placed by the side of some small rattan, as that of the palms.'—SEEMAN.

The rattan, or ratoung, which provides the canes of commerce, as well as the 'Penang Lawyers' and the Malacca canes, are all the produce of palms and not of bamboos. The bamboos are true gigantic grasses, and they come botanically about half-way between our common meadow-grasses and wheat and barley. They are very widely distributed, being found in large quantities in Asia and America, but there are none wild in Europe and only one in Africa. The family does not consist of so many species as the palms, but General Munro in his excellent monograph, published by the Linnæan Society in 1866, described one hundred and seventy species, which were increased in 1879 to two hundred and twenty species by Messrs. Riviere in their book, *Les Bambous*, a pleasant book specially devoted to the culture of the hardy bamboos.

Of these two hundred and twenty species perhaps a dozen or more may be described as quite hardy, and about as many more as doubtfully so, but all well worth growing. The first that was introduced as a hardy plant was, I believe, the *Thamnocalamus Falconeri*, from the Himalayas, one of the most elegant, though not the finest, and that was introduced about forty years ago. But it was not till the introduction of the Chinese and Japanese species that they were recognised as amongst the very best of hardy plants, and plants that perform a part in the garden which no other plants can. I cannot describe or even name all the hardy sorts. I find the hardiest are *B. metake* and *B. nigra*, and I think the most beautiful is *B. Castillonis*, which promises also to be one of the hardiest. It belongs to the section in which one side is flattened, and the flat side is a brilliant green, while the round portion is a golden yellow, forming quite a lovely combination both in form and colour. It is said to produce the four-sided shoot, so much used in Japanese furniture, and I find that many of the shoots on my plant are so, but not all. All the hardy sorts are most easy of cultivation when once established, but they dislike division and removal; and they are said to take root better when planted horizontally on the ground, with both stems and root covered, but I cannot speak of this from experience. They will bear heat or cold, drought or wet, and are not injured by wind; in fact, I know of no plants that give such an amount of beauty, and of usefulness too, with so little trouble. They seldom flower in England, and it is not desirable that they should, for the flowering is generally followed by death. This is well known in India, and the manner in which whole districts are laid bare has been often described; but in England I have never seen any in flower but the Himalayan *thamnocalamus*, which flowered about twenty years ago, not in one or two gardens only, but throughout England, and in many European gardens at the same time, and in every case of flowering the plant died.

It may be well to mention two fine hardy plants, to which the name of bamboo has been given. One is the false bamboo, *Arundo donax*, from South Europe and North Africa, a very grand bamboo-like plant, which is very hardy, and which has been a favourite in English gardens for nearly three hundred years, and of which the variegated form is perhaps the most beautiful of all the variegated plants, but not hardy. The other plant is the so-called sacred bamboo of Japan (*Nandina domestica*), which is not a bamboo at all, but is closely allied to the barberry, and is a most beautiful hardy shrub, and an especial favourite with Japanese gardeners and artists.

In one respect palms and bamboos may well be linked together. Wherever they are found they are each of them the most useful plants that grow. Their uses are in fact almost endless, and have been often enumerated. All I can say of them here is that it is well worth a visit to Kew, if only to see in the museum the many various uses to which palms and bamboos are put, and have been put from the earliest ages, while in the grand palm-house and in the open garden there is a collection of palms and bamboos such as no other European garden can show.

But in another respect palms rank far above bamboos. The bamboos have no literary interest, at least in English literature, while the palms have a surpassing interest. From the times of the Greeks and Romans (and probably earlier) the palm has been the accepted symbol of victory; and the reason given was that however much the palm-leaves are laden with heavy weights they do not break, and are with difficulty bent, and if bent at all they soon rise up again. I have seen this prettily illustrated in severe winters when the heavy snows have bent the tough leaves of the *Phormium tenax* so that they could not rise again; at the same time the large yuccas were rotted, and cedar branches broken, but the broad leaves of the palm carried the heavy load of snow, and immediately the snow was removed the leaves sprang up and the plants were quite uninjured. The old emblem writers made good use of this character in the palm; and Mary Queen of Scots took for her device a palm bending under a heavy weight, with the motto, 'Ponderibus virtus innata resistet.'

But it is from the Biblical references that the palm-tree has for us its chief interest. As we admire our palm-trees we think of the historical trees; of the seventy palm-trees that formed the pleasant oasis in the desert and marked the site of the refreshing wells; we think of the palm-trees of 'Jericho, the city of palm-trees'; of the palm-tree of Deborah; of the 'carved figures of palm-trees' that adorned the Temple, and especially of the palm branches that strewed the way in the triumphal entry into Jerusalem. And when we admire the beauty and majesty of the palm, we think how it is used as the type of all that is good and lovely:—

'I have never found in Holy Scripture' (says S. Francis de Sales) 'that the palm was made use of to represent anything but perfection, and it always serves as a similitude for high and excellent things.'

And so it is 'as the palm tree the righteous shall flourish', the beloved of the Canticles is 'of stature like a palm tree,' and, best of all, in the great vision the 'great multitude' of the redeemed were shown to the beloved disciple 'clothed with white robes and with palms in their hands.'

CHAPTER XXI

BRAMBLES AND THISTLES

Types of uselessness—Brambles in cultivation—Species of Thistles—Their edible qualities

When Milton published his scheme of 'A Compleat and Generous Education', he described the education then existing as a scheme by which

'We have now to hale and drag our chiefest and hopefullest wits to that asinine feast of sow-thistles and brambles which is commonly set before them, as all the food and nourishment of their tenderest and most docible age.'—*Of Education.*

In this way he showed his contempt for thistles and brambles, but he was, as usual, speaking more as a Biblical scholar than from personal knowledge of the plant. In the Bible, thistles and brambles are always spoken of as the proverbial types of bad husbandry, and the pests of cultivation, because throughout the Holy Land the general tendency of the native plants is to be thickly set with thorns, unpleasant both to the husbandman and to the traveller, so that Newton, writing in 1587 on the plants of the Bible, says no more than what later travellers have noticed, that

'Thystles, briers, and brembles, which grow out of the ground themselves, without planting or husbanding, yeelde in a manner no kind of commodity for the use of man, but rather detriment and annoyance both to man by their prickles, and to graine both by their ill company and neighbourhood.'

And so, having taken the palms and bamboos as types of all that is most beautiful and useful in the vegetable world, I will now take brambles and thistles as being the proverbial types of uselessness and annoyance.

But it is only as proverbial types drawn from Biblical associations that brambles and thistles are thus at once condemned, for as soon as we get away from Eastern and Biblical associations the case is changed. To begin with brambles. Without quoting many passages in which βάτος and *Rubus* are mentioned, and never in contempt, and without entering into the question how far they are identical with our bramble, I will only name one line in Virgil where he connects the bramble with the delicate *amomum*—

'Rubus et ferat asper amomum' (*Ecl.* iii. 89);

and one in Pliny—

'Neither hath Nature produced brambles for nothing els but to pricke and do hurt; but such is her bounty that the berries which they beare are man's meat, besides many other medicinable properties.'

And he gives a list of their virtues.

Clearly these writers did not despise the bramble, nor did our English ancestors; and while I claim for our wild bramble—'the scorned bramble of the brake'—that it is one of the most beautiful of our native plants, I claim also for the family at large that almost every species is well worthy of a place in the mixed garden. Our wild bramble, of course, must be kept out of the garden, or it will soon monopolise the whole, and we can admire its grace and beauty in any hedgerow, where it soon takes possession of every untidy corner; yet, though I think Walt Whitman's description, that 'the running blackberry would adorn the parlour of Heaven', is exaggerated, I should not object to it as a very lovely ornament of a garden if it were not for this 'running' quality. Many brambles, and our wild one especially, have the power and the habit of bending their shoots to the ground and there rooting, and so travelling and increasing at a very rapid rate. These long shoots rooting and then making fresh plants are strictly analogous to the runners or stolons of the strawberry, with which the bramble is closely allied; and for this reason they were (and perhaps still are) used for binding down graves, a custom which, though it had the sanction of Jeremy Taylor, can scarcely be recommended, as such a covering, unless very closely watched, would soon become a mass of untidiness. But if we cannot admit our wild bramble into our gardens, we may well admit it when it puts on variegated leaves. This it does in many different ways, and such brambles make beautiful bushes, which are easily kept in order; and there are two beautiful forms with double flowers, white and pink, which are exactly like branches of small roses, and flower in the autumn.

The family of the bramble is a large one, containing more than a hundred well-defined species, with a large number of varieties, being found in nearly all extra-tropical countries, though chiefly found in the northern hemisphere, and stretching from the extreme north in the Arctic Circle to the Falkland Islands in the south. Of these there are four distinct species in Great Britain, with many varieties of the common bramble; and it is my belief that of the whole number there is not one that is not beautiful either in foliage or flower or fruit. I will name a few which I should not willingly lose from my garden.

I think the finest of all is the Nutka Sound bramble (*R. Nutkanus*), with large leaves, and large, pure white flowers, looking like a fine single rose, and remaining in blossom a long time. (I need scarcely say that the brambles and roses are closely allied; even their names *Rubus* and *Rosa* are said to come from the same root, signifying *red*, and the most perceptible difference is in the fruit, which in the brambles is a fleshy, juicy fruit, borne on the calyx, and in the roses is the tube of the calyx itself, enlarged and coloured.) The *R. odoratus*, also from North America, is like the Nutka Sound bramble, but it is not so large, and the flowers are purple; it is more or less in flower all the summer. Both of these are thornless, and so is the *R. deliciosus* from the Rocky Mountains, with fine white flowers, but not, in my opinion, equal either in foliage or flower to *R. Nutkanus*. Of the high-growing brambles I should select two—the white-skinned bramble (*R. biflorus*), from Nepal, which, with its very white stems and leaves, is a striking object grown among other shrubs, and the red-haired bramble (*R. phoenicolasius*) from Japan, a very curious and beautiful plant. The flower is a poor one, but the long calyx-lobes and other parts are covered with red hairs ending in a gland, curiously like the sun-dew, and like that very destructive to small insects. The *R. laciniatus* is also a high-growing bramble, with beautiful leaves and fine black fruit, which the birds do not seem to fancy. Its native country is unknown, but it is said to be naturalised on Chislehurst Common and in parts of South Wales. Of the lower and more bushy brambles, the pink North American *R. spectabilis* would make a pretty bush if it had more flowers; but a far prettier little bush is the *R. rosæfolius*, which, though it comes from the East Indies and Mauritius, is perfectly hardy and has pretty double rose-like flowers. It flowers, however, so late in the autumn that in many years it does not flower at all, and I never saw the fruit, which in its native countries is said to be delicious. There are also a few low-growing prostrate brambles well worthy of a place in the garden. The Arctic bramble is remarkable for its fruit, which it only produces very sparingly in England, and indeed the plant is in most places difficult to establish; but in Sweden and Norway the fruit is produced in great abundance, and is largely used to make a very popular preserve. Very different and very curious is the Antarctic bramble (*R. australis*), which in New Zealand assumes many different forms; but in the form best known in England the trifoliate leaves are reduced to the three hard midribs, which, being thickly studded with delicate white thorns, give the whole plant a very pretty and uncommon effect.[1] To these two I should add a creeping bramble from the Himalayas, *R. nutans*, with handsome deep green foliage, and a single white nodding flower on an upright stem, very unlike any other bramble flower, and making an excellent plant for covering bare surfaces, even under trees.

I must not dismiss the brambles without some notice of the fruit, which in all the species is wholesome, and, as far as I know them, pleasant, and all more or less ornamental. If we had not the bramble in every hedge we should certainly grow it for the beauty and excellence of its fruit; and we may remember that the dewberry, which used to be considered a distinct species, but is now classed as a variety of the common blackberry, was considered by Shakespeare a fitting plant for Queen Titania to order for her love, and worthy to be placed with apricots, figs, grapes, and mulberries. The raspberry we have brought into our gardens, though it is a true native bramble, and by so doing we have improved the fruit, though in its wild state the fruit is excellent, and in some parts of England so abundant as to give quite a valuable harvest well worth gathering. Of late years the American

[1]In the variety with perfect leaves the thorns are black.

blackberries have been introduced into our gardens, but with very partial success. They seem to do well in some soils, and to bear good fruit, which comes in the autumn; but speaking generally, they have turned out failures, and even in America, where they are much cultivated, the latest report is 'that in our so-called improvement of fruits we have generally failed to improve the quality. Our most productive blackberries are large and beautiful, but they are inferior in flavour when compared with the wild ones found along the fence-rows of back pasture lots.' I have never succeeded in getting fine fruit on them, and the few I do get are always taken by the birds before they are fully ripe. And so I must leave the brambles, but not before I have quoted two stanzas from Eben. Elliott's pretty poem on the wild bramble:—

> 'Though woodbines flaunt, and roses grow
>   O'er all the fragrant bowers;
> Thou needst not be ashamed to show
>   Thy satin-threaded flowers—
>
> For dull the eye, the heart is dull,
>   That cannot feel how fair
> Amid all beauty, beautiful,
>   Thy tender blossoms are.'

I have left myself too small a space to speak of thistles as I should wish, for I think them as well worthy of admiration and cultivation as the brambles; and I mean by thistles all those members of the composite family which, though divided into many genera, have a common resemblance as having prickly stems, leaves, or flowers, with the flowers arranged in a more or less globular shape, and the sea-hollies and the teazel, which, though of different families, may well be ranged for our purpose in the same ranks. Of the thistles, we have in England four genera: the thistle proper (*Carduus*), the plume thistle (*Cnicus*), the cotton thistle (*Onopordum*), to which the thistle of Scotland is now generally referred, and the carline thistle (*Carlina*), and they are all beautiful in shape or colour, or both; and if it were not for their evil habit of producing abundance of seed, and scattering them in every direction by means of the exquisite thistledown, many of them would be welcome ornaments in any garden. As it is, I never pass the grand wayside woolly-headed thistle (*Carduus eriophorus*) without admiring the splendid foliage, which is almost equal to the classical acanthus, while the 'great, whitish, round, prickly head, flattish at the top, and thick set with wool, doth so well resemble the bald crown of a fryer, not only before it be in flower, but especially after it had done flowring, that thereupon it deservedly received the name of the Fryer's Crown Thistle' (Parkinson); and if I lived where goldfinches abound (but I do not), I should be tempted to grow thistles simply for the sake of the beautiful little birds to whom the thistles are so attractive. But I must confine myself to the garden species, and with something of the same apology that Parkinson felt compelled to make:—

'You may somewhat marvel to see me curious to plant thistles in my garden, when, as you might well say, they are rather plagues than pleasures, but when you have viewed them well what I bring in, I will then abide your censure.'

Among these I should select the different species of *Echinops*. These are well named from the echinus or sea-urchin, as, like that, the perfect flower-heads are exact globes set with spines; they are mostly European and perfectly hardy, and they are probably among the longest lived of any herbaceous plants. How long they will live and flourish in the same place I cannot say, but I have plants in my garden which I am sure have been in their present places for seventy years, and are as fresh and flourishing as if they had been planted this year. When fully perfect, the flowers are either blue or white, and 'they make a fine show, much delighting the spectator.' But their near allies, the *Eryingia*, are even handsomer. They are for the most part blue or white, and some of them, especially *Eryngium amethystinum* and *E. oliverianum*, are of a rich metallic blue colour both in flowers and stems, which I know of in no other flower whatever. All the *Eryngia* are handsome plants, most easy of cultivation, but there is one which I think is unsurpassed as a hardy plant where it likes the soil and is well grown. This is the *E. giganteum* from the Caucasus; it is only a biennial (as so many of the thistles are), but it sheds its seeds freely, and when once established in the garden is not easily lost. Its great beauty is in its second year, when it bears a large head of flowers which I can compare to nothing but a grand frosted-silver candelabrum. I know of no plant that is so attractive to strangers who see it for the first time, and it is a most attractive plant also to bees, both honey and humble bees.[1]

Having mentioned the edible uses of brambles, I may say that thistles also have their uses. The artichoke is a thistle, and I suppose was more esteemed by our forefathers than it is by us, for Evelyn says that shortly before his time they were 'so rare in England that they were sold for crowns apiece'; and as an ornamental plant it is a grand object planted singly on a lawn. Even the common thistles in Evelyn's day were in good repute, being 'about May sold in our herb markets, and is a very wholesome sallet eaten with oyl, salt, and pepper.'

Brambles and thistles do not sound likely subjects for a well-tilled garden, but I have specially chosen them as my subject because I believe there is no living organism that has not in it both beauty and interest, and among the vegetable organisms I believe there is none that may not with judgment be made to serve either to our use or pleasure, or both. The interest and beauty of any garden is not to be gauged by the amount of money spent upon it, and many a garden of homely and common hardy plants may give more pleasure to the owner, and be of more interest to visitors, than a grand garden which depends for its beauties on hothouses and conservatories and a host of gardeners. I once knew a man who was an excellent gardener and scientific botanist, who devoted a large part of his garden to docks. Of course he was laughed at, and his garden was called a dockyard, but it gave him much real pleasure, and he did good scientific work in it. I do not advocate the growth of docks, but I do think that our forefathers showed some wisdom in contenting themselves with 'a garden of simples,' and that even now, with all our wealth of flowers gathered from all quarters of the world, we need not despise such humble additions to our garden as we may find in brambles and thistles. The 'day of small things' still has its value—*inest sua gratia parvis*—and Chaucer's description of the 'poore persoun of a toun' (*i.e.* a parish priest) will also describe a good gardener who is content with something less than grandeur in his garden:—

'He cowde in litel thing have suffisance.'

[1]For a further account of thistles, see p. 60–1.

CHAPTER XXII

TREES IN THE GARDEN

Gardens in a wood—What trees to exclude—Cedars and Yews—Flowering
trees—Choice of situation

A GARDEN without trees scarcely deserves to be called a garden,
and if I had to build a house for myself, with, of course, a garden
attached, I have often thought that it would be very delightful to
build the house in an old wood, and gradually form the garden by
cutting it out of the wood. Such a thing has often been done. The
late Mr. Halliwell-Phillips built what he called a homely wooden
Bungalow in Hollingbury Copse, near Brighton, and made a
garden in the copse; but how far the garden was a success I do not
know. In a wood, at Wisley, near Weybridge, Mr. Wilson has
made a wood-garden, which has almost an European reputation;
but it is not a garden, it is still a wood, in which a large number of
plants are grown most successfully, and, as it is four miles from
the house, it certainly is not a home-garden, and I can only think
of a garden as an adjunct to a home. In America also it is not
uncommon for rich men to build for themselves a large house in
an uncleared forest, and to clear the forest only so far as to make it
a park in which the house stands. A small portion round the house
would be kept as a lawn, but this does not constitute a garden.
Trees by themselves will not make a garden. but a garden lacks
more than half its proper beauty if without trees; and so I propose
to talk of trees, what are and what are not suitable for gardens.

I should lay it down as a strict rule never to plant English forest
trees in a garden. If they are there already, there may be good
reasons for keeping some of them, but in a garden of limited
extent (and it is of such I am speaking) it seems a waste to plant
trees which can be had in perfection in the woods and hedgerows
outside of the garden, to the exclusion of the many fine exotic
trees which can only be grown in gardens. And even in retaining
British forest trees that may be on the ground, I think nothing can
be said for them unless they are of some special excellence. There

is perhaps no grander deciduous tree than the English oak, when
it has past its first manhood and is bordering on old age, and it
does seem cruel to cut it down. Yet it takes up too much room
when in its full grandeur, especially in certain soils. In some soils
it grows to a great height, with a clean straight stem, and not a
great spread of branches, as in the grand oaks at Bagot's Park, in
Staffordshire, and if it would always grow like that it might be
admitted into any garden, but the general habit is wide-spreading,
and I have seen an oak at Southgate, near London, of very
moderate height, but the branches cover a circle of which the
diameter is over 120 ft. There are very few gardens that could
admit such a tree.

On no account should an elm be admitted in or near a small
garden, though it is hard to exclude a tree which so rapidly takes a
beautiful shape, and which in the late autumn puts on such golden
tints. But probably no tree takes possession of a large extent of
ground so rapidly as this Italian stranger, for it is not a true native.
It sends up suckers at a considerable distance from the parent
tree, and these, if let alone, soon become trees. About forty years
ago a Scotch forester surveyed a part of South Devon to report on
the growth of hedgerow timber, and he reported that in the parish
of Clyst St. George the hedgerow elms occupied three-quarters
of the parish, for though only, or chiefly, in the hedgerows, their
roots extended so far into the fields that they met and even
overlapped in the middle of the fields, so that only one-quarter of
the parish could be considered free from the elm roots.

Beeches must be excluded, for nothing will grow under or near
them, and though the copper beech is much admired by many, I
could never like it. There are many different shades of copper
beeches, of which some may be less ugly than others, and for a few
days in the spring the colour of the young leaves is very brilliant,
quite equal to the Japanese maples, but a black tree is to my eyes a
monstrosity, and sufficiently ugly to justify Wordsworth's com-
plaint, that there were only two blots in his beautiful vale, a copper
beech and Miss Martineau. There is, however, one beech, the
fern-leaved, which makes a beautiful lawn tree, and has lovely
tints both in spring and autumn.

I dismiss at once the horse-chestnut, the sycamore (though, for a few days, when the flowers come out before the leaves, the whole tree is of a rich gold colour), the lime, the plane, and even the Spanish chestnut and the ash, as all better outside the garden than inside; but I would admit one upright poplar (and not more), for its unlikeness to everything around it, and a birch for its exceeding lightness and pretty bark. Of the other native deciduous trees I should be inclined to admit only the hornbeam. Though little grown as an ornamental tree, it makes, when not disturbed or clipped, a very beautiful lawn tree, with a very wide spread of branches which give a pleasant shade, the foliage not being too thick to admit glimpses of sun and light. The best sort is the hop hornbeam, with curious fruit exactly like hops, which are very ornamental, and remain on the tree a long time.

I am not fond of conifers in any part of a small garden; they are for the most part too formal in shape, too thick to give a pleasant shade, and too monotonous in colour. In a park or in large plantations they are very valuable, and in such places I can admire even the *Araucaria excelsa* (the puzzle-monkey), which when seen too near is the most artificial-looking tree in nature, the leaves and branches having almost a cast-iron texture. But there are two evergreen conifers which may be welcomed anywhere. The cedar of Lebanon is one, which (quite apart from its many associations, Biblical and otherwise) is the most delightful tree to grow on a lawn, and if it is in good soil it very soon takes a good shape, so that if I was limited to one tree I should choose a cedar of Lebanon. The deodar of the Himalayas, and the Atlas cedar are probably only geographical varieties, and are fine trees, but not equal to the cedar of Lebanon. The second evergreen conifer which I would not willingly be without is our own British yew-tree. I am not sure that I should plant one, for its growth is so very slow that it will scarcely give *nepotibus umbram*, and until it gets to a good age there is not much beauty in it; but I could scarcely cut down an old one. I am happy in having two old ones on my lawn growing near together, and far beyond the memory of the oldest inhabitant they have carried a swing, and it is pleasant to think to how many generations of the children of the village these yew-trees with their swing have been a never-failing delight. They are represented in an old painting quite two hundred years old. Besides these two evergreen conifers there are two deciduous ones, of which single specimens might claim a place. The larch, brought into England from the European Alps about two hundred and fifty years ago, is very beautiful in spring, and is almost the first of the deciduous trees that comes into leaf, and an old larch covered with lichen is a pretty sight; it is also one of the fastest-growing trees we have, and will grown anywhere. The *Salisburia*, or jingko-tree, from Japan (a near ally of the yew), is another deciduous conifer that should be on every lawn. It is very slow of growth in its earlier years, but its foliage (so like the maidenhair fern) is always pretty and interesting, and in a fine, dry autumn the autumnal tints are magnificent.[1]

I think we are all too shy of planting fruit-trees on our lawns. It is not easy to say why we should not plant apples, which bear (especially the pippins) such lovely flowers in great abundance, and which are equally if not more beautiful when covered with their fruit in autumn; as a summer tree there are certainly many more beautiful. The cherry-tree also is a delightful tree both in flower and fruit, and the autumnal tints are very rich, though not so rich in the cultivated as in the wild cherries, which in some counties, especially in Oxfordshire, are marked features in the woods and on some of the village commons, and in a mild autumn the leaves cling to the trees for a long time. For a short time in the spring the almond has a special beauty, but the flowers are very short-lived, and the tree is more suitable for a shrubbery than for a lawn.

But I must speak more of the many fine exotic flowering trees, which I said should be planted on our lawns in preference to our British forest trees. I suppose there is really no more beautiful flowering tree than the horse-chestnut, but I should not admit it into the garden; for though it has only been introduced about two hundred years, it has become one of our commonest hedgerow trees, and may be admired there; and although the foliage is very grand, the general outline and growth of the tree is too heavy and cumbersome for a lawn. But of all exotic flowering trees there are none to equal the magnolias. We generally grow them as shrubs,

[1] See p. 140–1.

or against a wall, but in many places they will grow, and not at all slowly, into fine trees. I remember one magnificent magnolia (I believe *M. grandiflora*) standing alone, and as large as a fine elm, near the old Roman Villa at Brading, in the Isle of Wight. This may be considered a favourable spot, but at Edgbaston Botanic Gardens, near Birmingham, which are in a very exposed and cold situation, there are some grand magnolias which may well take rank as forest trees. They are not the large-flowered species (*M. grandiflora*), but *M. acuminata*, *M. macrophylla*, *M. auriculata*, and *M. purpurea*, and the finest specimen of *M. acuminata* is nearly 50 ft. high, and 35 ft. through. The tulip-tree (*Liriodendron tulipifera*), from North America, is botanically closely allied to the magnolia, and is a most excellent lawn tree. Its large, quaintly shaped leaves, which in autumn turn to a rich yellow and brown, and its handsome, sweet-scented flowers, make it very attractive; it is also a rapid grower, and there are many trees in England from 100 ft. to 140 ft. high. The *Catalpa syringæfolia* is another beautiful tree for a lawn, allied to the bignonia, but with trusses of beautiful white and purple flowers, which are unlike any other flower. The drawback to it as a lawn tree is that it is so short a time in leaf. In a backward season the leaves will not appear till the end of June, or even the beginning of July, and will fall with the first frost; but as long as they last they are large and handsome, and the habit of the tree makes it a good tree for shade. The fruit is not often produced in England, but it is very curious, like a long French bean. I had abundance of seed in the Jubilee year, but never before or since; and in the same year the *Kohlreuteria*, from Japan, was also covered with handsome golden fruit. If this tree always produced its fruit I should recommend it, but it will only do so in such exceptional years, and so I do not recommend it for a small collection. Somewhat similar in foliage and even in flower to the catalpa (though not botanically allied) is the *Paulownia imperialis*, from Japan; but not so much to be recommended as the catalpa, because though a magnificent tree with beautiful purple flowers like a foxglove, the flowers come out before the leaves, and are seldom produced at all except in the mildest parts of England. For this reason I grow it as a shrub, or rather as a herbaceous plant, cutting it down to the ground every autumn. Under this treatment very strong shoots are produced in the spring, which carry throughout the summer immense leaves (I have measured them two feet across) of a very delicate colour and texture, so making one of the handsomest foliage shrubs I know.

It would be easy to make the list much larger, but I have in my mind a garden of a small extent, and for such the trees I have named would be almost sufficient. I do not mention such beautiful trees as thorns of many kinds, hollies. or service trees, because I should rather rank them as tall shrubs than as trees. But before I close the list I must mention two great favourites, which should be on every lawn, the medlar and the mulberry. I never saw a medlar that was not of a beautiful shape, and it makes a more natural tent or arbour than any other tree; the flower is handsome, and the fruit very acceptable to those who like it. Of the mulberry-tree we cannot say too much. The flowers are inconspicuous, but curious and well worth studying, and the fruit is delicious when we have a hot summer, and the tree is beautiful in shape and colour. An old mulberry-tree is an ornament to a lawn that any owner may be proud of, and it is so easily grown that large limbs cut off and stuck into the ground will grow. Among old gardeners it bore a very high character. Pliny though that

'It seemeth to have some sense and understanding, as if it were a living and sensible creature, for of all civile and domesticall trees it is the last that doth bud, and never before all the cold weather is past, and therefore she is called the wisest of all others.'[1]

Some may think that of the trees I have recommended a few only are suitable for all parts of England, while others are only fit for the warm sheltered situations of the south. But I believe they are all perfectly hardy anywhere if planted in proper situations, and a little attended to when young. I fancy that our forefathers were wiser than we are in their choice of situation for tender trees and shrubs. We are in the habit of putting them in the warmest corners we can find, while they chose the coldest. Leonard Mascall was a very practical gardener, and in 1590 he published

[1] In the P. B. version of the Psalms 'the mulberry-trees were destroyed with the frost'—but the translation is wrong; the tree named is the Sycomore.

A Booke of the Arte and Manner, How to Plant and Graffe all Sorts of Trees, etc., and this is his advice:—

'Commonly the most part of trees doe love Sunne at Noone, and yet the South Winde (or *vent d'aual*) is very contrary against their nature, and specially the almon tree, the Abricote, the Mulberie, the Figge tree, the Pomegranate tree.'

I am sure there is much in this. It is quite certain that all Japanese trees like shade and a north aspect; and the finest and most fruitful old mulberry-tree that I have ever seen is at Rochester, growing in a corner where it looks to the north and east, and is thoroughly protected from the south and west.

CHAPTER XXIII

BIRDS IN THE GARDEN

Sparrows—Birds and insects—Flying flowers—Garden music—The
Nightingale

IF I were to ask the question whether birds were useful or hurtful
in the garden, I should get many different answers. The pro-
fessional gardener would answer, without any hesitation, that he
would be glad to have them all cleared away. And certainly it is a
vexing thing to have to wage constant war with them, from the
sowing of the seed till the crops are gathered, and generally to be
beaten by them, for most of them have no respect for gardeners,
and no fear of any sort of scarecrows, or if they ever have a fear, a
very short acquaintance with the scarecrow soon breeds contempt, and they use it for a point of vantage. Yet there is much to
be said for the birds, even from the gardener's point of view, and,
without writing any general account of the birds that haunt, or
may from time to time be found, in our gardens, I wish to say
something for them, not only as beautiful additions to, but even as
helps in, our gardens.

Of all garden birds, I suppose the house-sparrow is everywhere
the most abundant, and it is not easy to say much in his favour. He
makes himself at home not only in the countries of which he is a
true native, but in America and Australia, to which he has been
taken by English settlers, he increases and multiplies till he has
become a subject of national importance; and wherever he is his
character is unaltered, he is everywhere the proverbial type of
boldness, impudence, and familiarity. His robberies in the garden
extend to almost everything, beginning with the flowers of the
crocus in the spring, and sparing nothing till he leaves the gardens
for the wheat-fields, where he literally takes tithe of the corn, for
his robberies are said to extend in some seasons to quite one-
tenth of the crop. Miss Ormerod, who is our great authority on
injury to crops by animals of all sorts, gives her verdict against the
sparrow in the strongest terms, and advises his wholesale destruc-

tion; and the old churchwardens' accounts, and the many sparrow clubs existing throughout the country for the express purpose of diminishing their number, if not of annihilating them, bear witness to the general belief that they are mischievous and useless. Yet I like the sparrow, and much may be said in his favour. His very impudence is attractive, and it is hard to say why the love for human society and human habitations should be condemned in the sparrow as impudent familiarity, and should be welcomed in the robin-redbreast as a charming confidence. Yet so it is, though it has not always been so. I suppose the Roman *passer* was our house-sparrow, and perhaps also the Greek στρουθός. It is now generally agreed that the sparrow of the Psalms and of the New Testament is not our sparrow. Yet it was so long identified with it in common belief, that it seems wonderful that the Psalmist's mention of it in connection with the holiest places, and still more our Lord's referring to it as a special object of the Father's love, should not have done as much in winning affection for the sparrow as the ballad of the 'Babes in the Wood' has undoubtedly done for the robin. But long before the 'Babes in the Wood' the sparrow had found his poet, and as long as sparrows are allowed to live among us, the two odes of Catullus, '*In passerem Lesbiæ*,' and '*Luctus in morte passeris*,' will plead something in his favour. And in spite of his mischievous habits there is much to be said for him. The amount of flies and other insects which he destroys is wonderful; and when we speak of the insects destroyed by the sparrows and other birds we must remember that most of them existed as caterpillars, and would be the parents of large families of caterpillars, and it is in the caterpillar stage that all insects are most destructive in the garden, and everything which can reduce the caterpillar in our gardens should be welcomed. My chief objection to the sparrows is the way in which they drive away other birds by taking possession of their nests. Swallows and martins are driven away by them in this way, and so far they must be condemned; but I will not say more about them, for I must go to other birds.

There may be some doubt about the usefulness of the sparrow in the garden; there can be very little about the thrush. I suppose our greatest enemies in the garden are slugs and snails, and the destruction which the thrush works among the snails at all times of the year is very great. How he finds them in their hiding-places is something of a mystery, but he makes no mystery of his method of destroying them; indeed, as he takes them to some well-seen stone, and there gives notice of what he is doing by his breaking the snails against it, he almost invites you to witness his work, and he seems so proud of it, and so conscious that he is doing good service, that for the time he lays aside his shyness and will let the gardener come very near looking watchfully at him, but not stopping in his work. And the thrush is, I believe, almost the only wild bird that does us this good service; ducks will eat a large quantity, but do mischief in finding them; and I know of no other bird that eats slugs, though hedgehogs eat them, and the shrew-mouse and the slow-worm are said to catch and eat many.

With the thrush, especially under his old names of 'the throstle, with his note so true,' who

> 'By breaking of the day
> Chants to his sweet full many a lovely lay';

or 'the mavis, that sings sweetly in the bush,' we always associate the blackbird:—

> 'The ouzel cock, so black of hue,
> With orange-tawny bill.'

They are closely connected: they are both lovers of gardens; they are both great robbers of strawberries, cherries, and, indeed, of all fruit that they can get at, but I claim for both of them that they earn much of what they rob by their constant destruction of insects and caterpillars, and both of them fully pay for the fruit they take from us by their unwearied power and beauty of song. But I have never seen the blackbird eating snails as the thrushes do, nor have I ever seen the starlings, though they are said to eat them; but the quantity of worms and insects that the starlings destroy must be very large, and they are beautiful objects on a lawn, in which they seem to take an especial delight, though their favourite hunting-ground is in the pastures in front of cows and horses, to whom they certainly do good service in freeing them from flies. At one time it was supposed that starlings were much diminishing in England, but they are in sufficient numbers now, and we could ill afford to lose them. In my own neighbourhood they roost in great flocks in a large wood, which is a well-known fox cover, and I am credibly informed that when they roost in the brushwood, which forms the larger part of the wood, the foxes catch them in large numbers.

It would be hard to guess at the number of flies that the different fly-catchers destroy every day. They are not afraid of man, and when they have a brood, both the parent birds will occupy some low branch or post within easy reach of their nest, and there, undeterred by any visitors, they will spend the whole day in catching flies and taking them to their nest. I cannot say anything now on the other fly-catching birds, as the robin, wren, swallows, swifts, etc., except that they are all useful and all beautiful. Of the larger birds, the cuckoo will at times come into the garden, and, I believe, never touches fruit; but the jay, the magpie, the rook, the jackdaw, and the wood-pigeon, are all inveterate thieves. The jay is now a scarce bird, except in very wooded districts, but the others are not only constant thieves, but generally confine their thefts to the very early morning before the gardeners are up, and at that time they manage to gather much booty; I believe a jackdaw will very soon strip a walnut-tree. Yet I should welcome them all, and am sure they do work which none but large birds can do, in the destruction of the larger caterpillars, and especially the wire-worm and the larva of the cockchafer.

But, allowing that the birds take toll of our fruits, and to a very large extent, can we do without them? William Lawson, in 1618, wrote of the '1000 delights that are in an orchard and garden,' and named as a special delight 'a broode of nightingales,' 'the gentle robin redbreast,' and 'the silly wren,' and added:—

'The blackbird and the threstle sing loudly on a May morning, and delighte the eare much (and you neede not want their company if you have ripe cherryes or berries), but I had rather want their company than my fruit.'

I do not agree with him; a little trouble in netting will do much to protect the fruit, and a garden without birds wants one of its best ornaments. I do not know who it was that called birds moving and flying flowers, but they may well be so called, and they are flowers that last in beauty all the year.

And their songs—can we do without them? Faber once addressed a poem to Cambridge, telling of its beauties and worth, but ending with 'Thou art a voiceless place; thou hast no bells'; but a voiceless garden, a garden without the singing of birds, is far more incomplete than a town without bells. It would scarcely deserve the name of a garden, certainly not of 'a pleasaunce,' or a paradise. Addison, writing to the *Spectator* (No. 477), in the assumed character of an eccentric or unfashionable gardener, describes his ideal garden:—

'My garden invites into it all the birds of the country by offering them the conveniency of springs and shade, solitude and shelter. I do not suffer any one to destroy their nests in the spring, or drive them from their usual haunts in fruit-time. I value my garden more for being full of blackbirds than cherries, and very frankly give them fruit for their songs. By this means I have always the musick of the season in its perfection.'

The perfection of such garden music where it can be had, and while it lasts, is the nightingale's; and of all song-birds none surpasses the English nightingale. Pliny gives an excellent description of the Italian nightingale, but when Philemon Holland translated it he showed his love of the English bird by a translation so free that it is not easy to detect in it much of the original Latin. The whole passage is delightful, but much too long to extract *in extenso*. I must, however, give the first part:—

'Is it not a wonder that so lowd and cleere a voice should come from so little a bodie? Is it not as straunge that she should hold her wind so long and continue with it as shee doth? Moreover, shee alone in her song keepeth time and measure truely; shee riseth and falleth in her note just with the rules of musicke and perfect harmonie; for the while in one entire breath she draweth out her tune at length treatable; another while she quavereth and goeth away as fast in her running points; sometimes shee makes stops and short cuts in her notes; another time shee gathereth in her wind and singeth descant between the plaine song; she fetcheth her breath againe, and you shall have her in her catches and divisions; anon all on a sodaine, before a man would think it, she drowneth her voice that one can scarce heare her, and then shee seemeth to record to herself, and then shee breaketh out to sing voluntarie. In summe, she varieth and altereth her voice to all keys; one while full of her largs, longs, briefes, semibriefes, and minims; another while in her crotchets, quavers, semiquavers, and demisemiquavers; for one time you shall heare her voice full and lowd, another time as low; and anon shrill and high; thick and short when she list, drawne out at leisure againe when she is disposed; and then (if shee be so pleased) she riseth and mounteth up aloft as it were with a wind-organ,' etc., etc., (x. 30).

A bird that gives us such music as this may not only plead for a place in our gardens for herself, but also for her fellow-birds, however mischievous they may be. And if we cannot have night-ingales we all have thrushes, and in one respect the song of the thrush is a greater addition to the garden than the song of the nightingale. The nightingale is with us for a very short time, the thrush is with us always, and his song not only lasts all day, and in summer far into the night, but he begins it again with the earliest dawn. This early song of the birds is, I think, one of the most charming of the mysteries of bird-life. A good hour before dawn the thrush sings out his morning song of praise, his *laudes matutinæ*, and then he seems to go to sleep again and not to wake till the sun has risen, and then he begins his full rich song, and continues at it more or less all the day. But I must say no more on the song of birds; the subject is much too large.

There is another side of the whole question. The American poet Emerson was once asked the use of the beautiful Rhodora growing in wild places far away from the sight of men. His answer was:—

'Why thou art there, thou rival of the rose,
  I never thought to ask, I never knew,
But in my simple ignorance suppose,
  The self-same Power that brought me here, brought you,'

The longer I live, and the more I study my garden, the more I feel the truth that underlies the poet's words. He is a bad gardener whose garden is kept only for himself. Paradise was not made for Adam only, but for 'every beast of the field and every fowl of the air that was brought unto him' there. And we add largely to the pleasure of our gardens when we look on them not only as pleasant homes for our flowers and fruit, but also as the homes of many lovely and interesting living creatures. We cannot spare the birds, though we may have to pay largely for their beauty and their song. We cannot spare the butterflies and moths, though as caterpillars they are most destructive. I should be sorry not to have the little spider which weaves such a net-work of beauty on our shrubs in the early autumn mornings; and even our greatest enemies, the slugs, snails, and mice, which may be caught and killed without mercy, add to the interest of our garden, and most assuredly, though we may not see it, they have their use.

CHAPTER XXIV

GARDEN ASSOCIATIONS

Plants with Biblical interest—Historical associations—Plant literature—
Scents—Legends

I THINK that February is almost the most interesting month of the year to the gardener: in no other month are there so many changes. Every day, and almost every hour, shows some old favourite coming to cheer and delight us with the same beauties as before, and yet not the same; and as I go round the garden, I often try to puzzle out some of the mysteries of the long sleep and the awakening of plants, and always with the same result, that it is all a mystery which hitherto has utterly defied our research.

Everything connected with the sleep of plants is full of interest, and especially the sleep during hard frost, for we are very ignorant of the action of frost on plants, we cannot say for certain how the destruction begins or ends, nor can we in any way tell from the structure of a plant that it will or will not be able to resist frost. We can speak learnedly of the bursting of cells, and the breaking up of protoplasm, but that only puts the question one step further back: it explains *ignotum per ignotius*, and no more; and until the impossible man comes who can understand all mysteries and all knowledge, it will always remain a mystery, and one of the chief charms of a garden is that it is a great storehouse of mysteries.

I have heard gardeners say that a plant is not worth growing unless it has beauty of flower or foliage or scent. I should say that many plants are worth growing for several other reasons, such as botanical or historical interest. I would not willingly be without the green rose, or the four-petalled Himalayan rose (*R. sericea*), or the Plymouth strawberry, or the one-leaved strawberry (*Fragaria monophylla*), for though none of these have any special beauty to recommend them, they have great botanical interests. But the great charm of many flowers lies in their associations, which of course vary with different people, but there are some which are common to all. It is of these associations that I wish to speak in this paper.

Foremost among such plants I place all that have a Biblical interest. I have often had the pleasure of taking round my garden parties of mechanics, young men's associations, school teachers, etc., the greater part of them without any botanical or horticultural knowledge, and I always find that no plants interest them so much as the plants of which they have read in the Bible. The Christ's thorn (*Paliurus aculeatus*) deeply interests them. Whether it is really the plant of the crown of thorns may be doubtful, but few other plants so well satisfy the requirements; and when I show them the pliant branches so easy to weave into a crown, and so thickly set with sharp thorns in every direction, they generally show their interest by asking for pieces to take away with them. Abraham's oak (*Quercus pseudo-coccifera*) is another plant almost as interesting, and the terebinth was another, but this is somewhat tender, and I have lost if for many years. Other plants of Biblical interest which I grow are the cedar of Lebanon, the palm, the fig, the olive, the willow of Babylon, the styrax (supposed to be the poplar of the Old Testament), the pomegranate, the mandrake, hyssop, and spikenard, the almond and the quince.

Other plants have historical associations. The white rose of York, the Irish shamrock, and the Scotch thistle, are instances; and the broom of the Plantagenets; the Alexandria laurel, which formed the crown of the Greek conquerors; the acanthus, which gave the model to the Corinthian capital; the papyrus of Egypt (not hardy), get their chief interest from their historical associations. Other plants have a commercial and officinal interest, but to write of these would be quite beyond the limits of a short paper; others have a geological interest, and others a geographical. By plants of geological interest I mean plants that are strictly limited to particular strata, like our Cornish heath, which clings to the serpentine formation; and by plants of geographical interest I mean plants that are specially interesting from their localities as wild plants, such as the American plants which have found a home for themselves on the west coast of Ireland, or the Spanish plants on the south coast. It is very pleasant to be able to show growing together the Antarctic bramble with its curious skeleton leaves and white thorns, and the Iceland poppy from the Arctic Circle, which is reported to be the most northern flowering plant known,—so extremely northern that I was told by one of the officers in the North Pole expedition, that if there was land there he should expect to find the Iceland poppy.

Even the names of plants supply many associations, and in this respect, I think, plant growers are more fortunate than students of some other natural sciences (say, for instance, entomology), because the names often supply much information either of the structure of the plant or its native locality, or its discoverer. Thus, Winter's bark (*Drimys Winteri*) will not only recall Admiral Winter's great voyage of discovery round Cape Horn and through the Straits of Magellan, where the shrub was found, but it will also recall something of the history of Cinchona, for which it was long a substitute. But plant names form too fascinating and lengthy a subject to enter on here.

An endless amount of interest is gathered round the literary history of plants. I like to grow any plant that is mentioned by the old Greek and Latin writers—such as Theophrastus, Aristotle, Virgil, or Pliny; and still more do I delight in the plants of English literature. I doubt if any national literature has been so full of flowers as our own, and especially in our poetry. Among the older writers, Gower, Chaucer, Spenser, and Shakespeare, and, indeed, almost all, love to speak of gardens and flowers. The plants named by them are far more than most people are aware of, and a very slight acquaintance with their writings will add much to the pleasure of a garden. And this love of gardens and flowers was not confined to the older poets; it rather languished in the eighteenth century, but in our day flowers have been fully honoured by our poets. Of course, modern poets have naturally loved the old flowers, but they have not hesitated to speak lovingly also of the newer introductions. The latest addition to the flora of the poets is the yucca, and, as I have always grown this plant largely, I am glad to see it so honoured. I wonder it has so long remained unsung, for it was a very early introduction from the New World, and was grown in England by Gerard in 1597; yet, as far as I know, no poet has noticed it before the late poet-laureate, and he has done so in his latest work:—

'My Yucca which no winter quells,
   Although the months have scarce begun,
   Has pushed towards our faintest sun
A spike of half-accomplished bells.'

To Ulysses. Demeter, p. 113.

It is a well-known fact that nothing recalls the past like scents, and this is so especially true of the scent of flowers, that I suppose most of us can name instances in our own experience. I never gather a leaf of the fine-leaved form of the oak-leaf geranium without at once going back in memory to a pleasant home in the Midlands, where the genial host was so fond of the leaf that it always formed a part of the 'button-hole' of his guests. Elwanger, in *The Garden's Story*, carries this too far when he says that the 'perfume of *Lilium auratum*, stealing from the spotted petals, recalls the reedy jungle and the spotted tiger.' Mr. Savage Landor says more truly—

'Sweet scents
Are the swift vehicles of still sweeter thoughts,
And nurse and mellow the dull memory,
That would let drop without them her best stores.'

But best of all was the excellent use that the late Miss Hope, of Edinburgh, made of her sweet-scented flowers. She was indefatigable in providing comforts for the sick in hospitals, and among the comforts she included a plentiful supply of flowers, but with the proviso that the flowers should be common flowers, and always accompanied with a sprig of some woody, aromatic plant, for the special purpose of recalling memories of home.

Of all the associations which flowers keep for us, none can equal those connected with persons or places. Of the way in which flowers bring back the memory of friends little can be said; in the pleasure they thus bring they must vary according to the memories they recall, and in not a few cases these memories may be full of sadness and sorrow. But the memories of places which flowers bring back to us must always, I think, be more or less pleasant; and to pick flowers or to collect plants in various places, and then to be able to grow them in our own gardens, adds much to the pleasure of travelling. My beech-fern recalls Cader Idris to me, and my oak-fern Snowdonia, though it is many years since I collected them; and my Osmunda recalls North Donegal and Slieve League, not because my plants come from there, but because I never saw them elsewhere so beautiful; my saxifrages recall Switzerland, and my pinks the Castle of Falaise; my pulsatilla recalls the beautiful hillside near Thring, which I once saw studded with the flower in a luxuriance that I fear is now a thing of the past; while my sedums recall a pleasant afternoon in the Botanic Gardens at Angers, where the pleasant old curator, M. Boreau, made that family his special study, and gave me an excellent collection; and as to other gardens, both public and private, they are recalled to me most pleasantly in almost every yard of my garden. And these associations have what I may call a reflex character that doubles the pleasure. I can remember my delight when I first saw the beautiful *Campanula barbata* in the Swiss valleys; it had always been a special favourite with me as a garden beauty; and now, when I see it, I call to mind a delightful walk up the Flegère, where this lovely flower grows in the greatest abundance, in all shades of white and blue, from the commencement of the ascent in the valley of the Arve till the pine woods are passed. Tennyson records the same double pleasure brought to him in connection with one small flower:—

> 'We took our last adieu,
> And up the snowy Splugen drew,
> But ere we reached the highest summit,
> I plucked a daisy, I gave it you;
> It told of England then to me,
> And now it tells of Italy.'

And these memories and associations that our flowers give us are independent of seasons or of age. They come to us as well in autumn and winter, in spring and summer; and as to age, the older we get the more, from the very nature of things, do these memories increase and multiply.

I have said nothing of the legendary associations of flowers, they are too numerous; but I will just name the forget-me-not, that with it I may bring this paper to a close. All admire the pretty flower, and like to tell of the pretty, though modern, legend. But in my garden, and I know it is the same in the gardens of all who love flowers, nine-tenths of my plants and flowers are forget-me-nots, and have their legends, which they tell to me over and over again, and which I often like to repeat to others. There are trees on my lawn which were planted when children were born; there are hundreds of plants which tell me of the liberal help given by such gardens as Kew, Edinburgh, Dublin, and many other public gardens, both British and foreign; there are hundreds of others which speak to me of delightful private gardens, and of the pleasant freemasonry that exists among true gardeners; there are flowers which tell of pleasant travels, and long walks, and beautiful spots which I shall probably never see again; there are others which bring to memory voices which I shall never hear, and faces which I shall never see again in this world; and hundreds more which in their several ways have their own memories, and their own associations, which make each and all forget-me-nots of the highest value and beauty. And in looking on our flowers with these thoughts there is nothing mawkish or sentimental, the thoughts are good and wholesome; and though some of the memories connected with our flowers may be sad, and some of the associations may be even painful, yet *meminisse juvat* is written upon them all; and that our flowers can give us such memories. and can be linked with such associations, we may, indeed, be thankful.

CHAPTER XXV

GARDEN LESSONS

Laws of the plant-world—Our ignorance—One touch of nature—The
economy of nature

THE lessons which can be learned from flowers are almost as
numerous as the flowers themselves; quite as numerous, if, as I
believe, every plant has its own separate message and lesson. Into
these, of course, I cannot enter, I can only point out a few which
are more or less taught by all, and I leave out all spiritual and
religious lessons, for I am not writing a 'Flower Sermon.'

The great lesson that our gardens teach us is, that everything in
nature is subject to the strictest law, for this is taught by plants
almost more surely than by anything else; because most living
organisms, such as men and animals, having powers of moving,
and of exercising will, thought, or instinct, can change their
surroundings, and so in many cases can change their special
characters. But the plant-world is governed by strict, unchanging,
and, we may say, eternal laws. What I mean is this:—If I take two
sets of small seeds in my hands, they may at first sight seem
absolutely the same, yet one may be the seed of a small annual, the
other the seed of a large tree; and if I know the history of the plants
that produced the seeds, I can foretell with certainty the whole
future life of the seeds, the shape and nature of the leaves, the size
of the plants, the colours of the flowers, the shapes and uses of the
fruit, and the length of life which will be allotted to each. Every
plant that grows is produced and lives by the strictest law; like has
produced like from the beginning, and will do so to the end. And
this is so perfectly true, that there can be no doubt that the flowers
we admire now are identical with those which were grown by
Greek and Roman, Egyptian or Assyrian gardeners, identical in
every respect, shape, colour, foliage, and scent. Keble carries the
idea to its furthest limit, and identifies his own 'sweet nurslings of
the vernal skies' with the flowers of Paradise:—

'Relics ye are of Eden's bowers,
  As pure, as fragrant, and as fair
As when ye crowned the sunshine hours
  Of happy wanderers there.
....

Your first and perfect form ye show,
The same that won Eve's matron smile
  In the world's opening glow.'

But though the laws of plant-life are so strict that it is impossible for a plant to grow except in obedience to the laws, yet, within certain limits, it is possible for man to produce changes, or for the plant itself to show varieties, which may be more or less permanent, and it is to these changes and variations that we owe many of our most beautiful garden flowers. But the limits of varieties are strictly defined, and however many varieties may be produced, the original typical plant goes on just the same. The wild potato on the coast of Chili is the same that was found in the sixteenth century. The wild scarlet pelargonium, from which our numberless varieties have sprung, may still be found at the Cape. And so strict are the limits of variation, that in spite of all efforts, these two plants have never become in the least degree hardier than when first introduced, and probably never will be; and though the gardeners have so much altered the pelargonium that it is now a flower with five almost equal petals, yet the original irregular form cannot be entirely obliterated, and the one larger petal of the typical plant is always shown by the curious hole at the base, which no hybridising has completely destroyed, but the use of which has never been satisfactorily accounted for. Some of these variations are so different from the parent type that they used to be ranked as monstrosities. They are no longer so ranked, for one of the good services which Darwin did for the natural sciences was to show us that there are no such things in nature as monstrosities. What are called by that name are only hints of the possibilities of nature, and are even proofs of the strict laws under which plant-life exists, for these monstrosities never go beyond well-defined limits, and in course of time often revert to the parent type. And that this was so had not escaped the notice of other deep thinkers before Darwin. Nearly two hundred years before, Isaac Barrow, in his twelfth sermon on the Creed (a sermon well worth the study of all students in natural science), said—

'That which we call a monster is not unnatural in regard to the contexture of causes, but arises no less methodically than anything most ordinary; and it also hath its good end and use, well serving to illustrate the beauty and convenience of nature's usual course.'

And he quotes Aristotle— ουδέν γίνεται παρὰ φύσιν.

Another excellent lesson which my garden teaches me is my own ignorance. I once asked one of our most learned botanists a simple question about some flowers. His answer was, 'I cannot tell you, and I have come to the conclusion that I know nothing whatever about flowers.' A few days after I asked another friend's advice about a plant that was not doing well. His answer was, 'Oh yes, I can tell you all about it; I can tell you at once what is the matter with a plant.' I very soon reached the bottom of his knowledge, or rather of his ignorance. As I walk round my garden, I read in every plant my own ignorance of its real history. Take the flowers now so popular, and so beautiful, the hellebores, or Christmas roses. The pure white flower is not, as it seems to be, the corolla, but the sepals of the calyx. The true petals are curious little things shaped like trumpets, set round the ovaries, and soon falling off. The petals of the yellow aconite are the same, and by old writers they were called nectaries; and if by nectary is meant the part which holds the bait that attracts the insects, the name is a good one. Both hellebores and the winter aconite belong to the same great family of *Ranunculaceæ*, but in no other member of the family, and as far as I know in no other family, do we find these trumpet-shaped petals. What can be their special use in the economy of the plant I cannot say; I can only guess that as these plants come into flower always in cold weather, and often in the depth of winter, a special protection for the 'nectar' might be required, and would be given by these little trumpets; but this is the merest guess. To one, however, who wishes to puzzle out a difficult but not unpleasant subject, I would recommend the study of the petals of the *Ranunculaceæ*. It is a very large family, and is not a difficult one; but throughout the family the petals are curious, running as they do through the no-petals of the clematis, the bright petals of the buttercups, and the quaint petals of the columbines, larkspurs, and monkshoods. I have one small piece in my garden, in which I delight to puzzle my botanical friends. Close together I have three plants growing, each of which has its puzzle. There is the *Galanthus scharloki*, a poor snowdrop, but very interesting to me, because, instead of having a simple spathe, and one pure white flower, as all snowdrops should have, it has a two-leaved spathe, and sometimes two flowers, and a green external spot, so coming near to a snowflake. Next to it is *Heuchera* or *Tolmiæa Meiziesü*, from North America, a plant of no great beauty, but also interesting, because, besides increasing by seeds or offsets as all the rest of the family does, it produces young plants in abundance on the top of each leaf. And next to that is *Acæna pulchella*, an excellent little trailer for covering banks. The fruit of all the *Acænas* are burs; but they all differ in their special ways of clinging to the passer-by. In *Acæna microphylla* the little thorns are sharp, simple points. In some of the others they are hooks, but in *Acæna pulchella* they are beautiful little arrows with double barbs. Now, in all these three plants there is a hidden history which would tell us what there was in the original surroundings that caused these differences and has perpetuated them; but the history is a hidden one, and so must remain, and when any one tells me that he knows all about plants, I have but to show him some little and apparently such insignificant points as these, and the most learned at once confess their ignorance.

Another lesson which the garden teaches is how nearly connected we all are with every other living organism. This is a very large and a very deep subject, which I am quite unable to enter into fully, and it is difficult to state even the slight hints of it that the garden gives. That there is between human life and plant life something closer than and different to the simple connection between the cultivator and the crop seems to have been felt by many. Something of the sort must have been in Shakespeare's mind when he said, 'One touch of nature makes the whole world kin,' which is not, as generally quoted, a mere platitude about benevolence, but, as the whole passage shows, is a statement of the relationship existing between all parts of nature, or, as Wallace puts it—

'The forces of life appear to be fundamentally the same for all organisms, as is the material of which all are constructed; and we thus find behind the outer diversities an inner relationship which binds together the myriad forms of life. Each species of animal or plant thus forms part of one harmonious whole.'— *Darwinism*, c. xi.

Wordworth felt this very strongly, affirming that flowers laughed, and showed gladness or sorrow as much as he did himself. Longfellow had the same feeling, and, speaking of 'the stars of earth, those golden flowers,' he said—

'In all places then and in all seasons
  Flowers expand their light and soul-like wings,
Teaching us by most persuasive reasons
  How akin they are to human things.'

Many will find it difficult to realise this; but I think all who love flowers and live much amongst them have felt how flowers seem to sympathise with their own feelings, how different they look when all is bright and happy to what they look when sorrow and trouble are upon us, and I think that the old bell motto is really true of flowers, 'Gaudemus gaudentibus, dolemus dolentibus.'

But I must leave this subject, only thus touching its fringe, for one more commonplace. I learn from flowers the perfect usefulness of every part of creation. I do not mean the usefulness to man only, measured by what it can buy him in comforts or in pounds, shillings, and pence, but I mean that every created thing has its own allotted place in the world, and fills the particular place which it fills better than anything else could. People who are not gardeners look on botany as an abstract science of no great practical use, but even in the matter of commercial utility the results are really very striking. In Mr. Jackson's *Commercial Botany of the Nineteenth Century*, recently published, there is a long and most interesting list of plants of different sorts that have been introduced into commerce during the present century, and of nearly all of them there is the record of most material assistance given by the scientific staff at Kew. But this is not all; plants which apparently are of no use to man, and plants which are even hurtful to man, have yet their uses in the economy of nature; and it is no proof to the contrary that we have not yet been able to find them out. We have only to think of the hundreds of thousands of square miles on the globe's surface where man never comes, but which are covered with the full vegetation suitable to each part, and we soon realise that plants must have their uses though no man sees them. On this subject I cannot do better than again quote Isaac Barrow:—

'Everything contributes somewhat to the use and benefit or to the beauty and ornament of the whole; no weed grows out of the earth, no insect creeps upon the ground, which hath not elegancy and yields not its profit; nothing is abominable or despicable, though all things are not alike amiable or admirable.'—*Sermon on the Creed*, x.

And very much to the same effect, Friar Laurence, in *Romeo and Juliet*, describes the 'baleful weeds and precious-juicèd flowers' which he is going to gather—

'Many for many virtues excellent,
None but for some, and yet all different.
O mickle is the powerful grace that lies
In herbs, plants, stones, and their true qualities;
For nought so vile that on the earth doth live
But to the earth some special good doth give.'

CHAPTER XXVI

PARSONAGE GARDENS—AD CLERUM

*Parsons and plants—Parishioners and their Parson—The pleasures
of Botany—The Manse garden*

I OFTEN regret that George Herbert did not add another chapter
to his *Country Parson*, and tell us his views of the parson in his
garden. With his high views of the importance of the parson's
character showing itself in the minutest details of daily life—'he
leaveth not his ministry behind him, but is himself wherever he
is'—it would have been pleasant to have been taught by him how
the parson could manage his garden, not only 'in the knowledge of
simples, wherein the manifold wisdom of God is wonderfully to
be seen,' but also 'like a parson, thus raising the action from the
shop to the Church.' That he had not only a love of flowers and
gardening, but also a full knowledge of them, is shown by many
passages in his poems; and in the chapter on 'The Parson's
Completeness' he considers a knowledge of plants to be necessary in a parson—that he would be incomplete without it.

And a country parson without some knowledge of plants is
surely as incomplete as a country parsonage without a garden.
Certainly he deprives himself of much pleasure, and in some
respects of usefulness. I am thankful that my own lot has been cast
for me in the country, yet I can fully understand and appreciate
the actual pleasure which an active earnest clergyman finds in the
crowded, unlovely streets, and even in the slums of a densely
populated city cure, and I can even sympathise with his dislike to
the quiet stagnation (as he would call it) of a country parsonage;
but I cannot understand a clergyman whose lot has been cast in
the country, and who has accepted the lot, shutting his eyes to all
the beauties which surround him and which come up to his very
doors, and to whom the change of seasons, and even the changes
from day to day that he must see, are only changes from one kind
of dulness to another. Such a man must be wretched in a country
parsonage, but I have not much pity for him.

I need not describe the ideal English parsonage and its garden. It has been described over and over again, and indeed it has passed into a proverb, so that when a house is described as 'like an ordinary English parsonage,' as Wordsworth's home is described, we know at once what it means. We picture to ourselves a building of moderate size—not pretentious—neither a mansion nor a suburban villa (*Parva sed apta domino* is the inscription on an old Wiltshire parsonage), and of an old foundation; yet with many additions and accretions of different dates, each bearing some impress of the successive owners; and the garden is of the same character, often standing (and always in the ideal parsonage garden) near the church and churchyard, so that the church forms the feature in the garden. The parsonage garden is not large, seldom exceeding two acres, and more often not exceeding one, with little glass, and no pretension to a high-class garden, but with a good spread of old lawn and many old trees and flowering shrubs, all suggestive of repose and quiet, pleasant shade, and freedom from the bustle of the outside world. The parsonage garden some years ago was a home for hundreds of good old-fashioned flowers, but I am afraid no gardens suffered more from the bedding craze, which swept them clear of all their old long-cherished beauties, and reduced them to the dull level of uniformity with their neighbour's gardens, or to miniature mockeries of Trentham or Clieveden. That craze has to a great extent passed away, and the parsonage gardens are gradually recovering their old features, and fortunately they are able to do so more easily than some other gardens, because in most of them the trees and shrubs were spared, and have been a valuable help in the restoration to a better and more healthy style of gardening, and one more in keeping with the character of the country parson's garden. There are hundreds of such good old gardens scattered throughout England, of which Charles Kingsley's garden at Eversley and White's garden at Selborne are well-known typical examples.[1]

That such gardens are a real pleasure and refreshment to the

---

[1] White's garden at Selborne was a typical parson's garden, but it was not the real parsonage.

owners we all know, and they are none the less so when the refreshment is taken in hard manual labour, for many a country parson can bear witness that 'the very works of and in an orchard and garden are better than the ease and rest of and from other labores' (William Lawson, 1608). But I said also that parsonage gardens had their usefulness, by which I mean they may be made useful to the clergyman in his parochial work. How this may be done I need not say at any length, because the method that would be very useful in the hands of one would be perfectly useless in the hands of another. I would only say generally, that the love of flowers and gardening is so universal amongst the English peasantry that a country parson will often find a better introduction to a cottager through his garden than by any other means. And though the love of flowers is so universal, and the garden may be such a useful adjunct to the cottage, yet there is very great ignorance of the right principles of gardening, and the parson may be of great use to his poorer neighbours, not only by teaching, but still more by showing them better ways in his own garden. For the parsonage garden gate should be always open, and every parishioner welcomed; there need be no fear of any undue advantage being taken of the free permission to enter—the one difficulty will be to induce them to come in. And the parson may do much to brighten the gardens of his parish, and so to increase the interest in them by giving plants from his own garden. I have for many years been a cultivator of hardy plants, and have been able to gather together a large number of species; and I was long ago taught, and have always held, that it is impossible to get or keep a large collection except by constant liberality in giving. 'There is that scattereth, and yet increaseth,' was Solomon's experience, and it certainly is so with gardening; and the parson who is liberal with his plants will find the increase not only in the pleasant intercourse with his neighbours, but also in the enlargement of his own garden, which thus spreads beyond his own fences into the gardens of the cottages. Some clergy can do more than this by giving actual instruction in the wonders of plant-life, as was done some years ago most successfully by Mr. Henslow, and also by Mr. Dawes, the Dean of Hereford, who gave object-lessons in his garden at King's Somborne; but this requires a special knowledge, and these two men were specially gifted with great knowledge, and with the happy power of imparting their knowledge to others.

There is one way in which I am sure the country parson might make his garden useful to himself in his minsterial work:—

'I am not in the least ashamed' (says the Rev. John Laurence in *The Clergyman's Recreation* in 1714) 'to say and own that most of the time I can spare from the necessary care and business of a large parish, and from my other studies, is spent in my garden, and I cannot but encourage and invite my reverend brethren to the love of a garden, having myself all along reaped so much fruit both in a figurative and literal sense.'

The figurative fruits are the spiritual lessons he had learned from his flowers and garden; and I think the old writers and the old gardeners were more alive to these lessons than we are now. St. Francis de Sales was very fond of drawing his illustrations from flowers, and his notices of flowers and their lessons have been collected into a 'Mystical Flora.' Joachim Camerarius, an excellent botanist, published in 1590 a *Centuria of Emblems* from plants; and with its pretty plates and excellent scholarly and religious descriptions it makes a charming little volume. In 1657 Ralph Austin, 'practiser in the art of planting,' published *The Spiritual Use of an Orchard or Garden of Fruit Trees set forth in divers similitudes between Natural and Spiritual Fruit Trees*, in which, though the similitudes are often far-fetched, and the lessons strained, there is much that is well worth reading; and a little later was Flavel's excellent little book of a similar character, *Husbandry Spiritualised*. In our own day, *The Catholic Florist* (1851) is a pleasant little book on the spiritual lessons of flowers, and their association with different saints and saints' days, though sadly marred by fictitious quotations; and later still we have had similar lessons pleasantly taught to us by Mrs. Gatty and Mrs. Ewing.

Much might be said on the great pleasures that the science of botany will give to a country life, and much more might also be said on the special advantages of a knowledge of the science and the practical uses of a garden to the country parson, but I will content myself with some words of others who have written on the subject. I have already mentioned *The Clergyman's Recreation* by

Laurence. It is a good little book, but except in the Preface has little specially for the clergy. The Preface is, however, written *ad clerum*:—

'To recommend the art of managing a garden to those of my own order, the clergy, not to make them envied by magnificence, but to make them happy by loving an innocent diversion suitable to a grave and contemplative genius. . . . This I suppose most people will allow, that as there are some sports and exercises not suitable to a divine, so gardening is a very agreeable and com-mendable recreation—viz. pruning, planting, sowing, grafting, and inoculating, and sometimes digging, *ad ruborem*, but not *ad sudorem*.'

In 1796 *Three Dialogues on the Amusements of Clergymen* was published, professing to be the views of Bishop Stillingfleet, communicated to Dr. Josiah Frampton. It is rather an amusing book, and can scarcely be taken seriously, but is quite worth reading. All amusements are more or less forbidden, except battledore and shuttlecock in the tithe barn. Gardening naturally forms one of the subjects of discussion, and he has little to say about it except that 'there cannot be a more clerical amusement,' but he gives the good advice that the clergyman should try to make his garden the best in the parish, a model garden to his neigh-bours.

But the best book on clerical gardening is *The Manse Garden*, a book published nearly seventy years ago, and now, I believe, out of print, but well worth reprinting. The author was the Rev. N. Paterson, at that time minister of Galashiels, and afterwards a leading member of the Scotch Free Kirk. It is altogether a delightful book, full of quaint sentences, shrewd good-sense, and quiet humour, and the cultural directions are admirable. I men-tion it more particularly here because throughout the book the clergyman is never lost sight of, and though written for Scotch ministers and Scotch manses, it is equally suitable for English country parsons and country parsonages. The one chapter on 'The Minister's Boy,' which concludes the book, will come home to many an English country parson. There are many passages which I should like to extract showing the pleasant humour and practical character of the book, but I must content myself with one in his more serious strain, as having a closer reference to my subject, and showing something of the ministerial aspect of the book:—

'You will find in the very nature of the work a new interest communicated to your life, and which, relieving the pressure of cares and lightening the burden of toil, will tend to no worldliness of spirit. Thus conferring as well as receiving good, and incurring no evil, let our gardens and every corner of our glebes be adorned; and if we have to lament, on the part of those having large possessions, that too little is done, let us at least set an example, though it be but in the model style, and have our home a paradise of fruit and flowers, of shelter and shade, endeavouring still to make the place the more worthy of ourselves, and ourselves more worthy of the place.'

One point must not be left unnoticed. It seems almost unnatural for a country clergyman to be without some love of flowers and gardens; and the study of them comes recommended not only as a refreshment and from its practical usefulness, but also for its scientific and literary associations. Yet it has its snares, of which the chief is that it may become too interesting and too absorbing. Its very innocence may help on and even conceal the snare; but the snare is there as it is in everything else in this world, however good, and I never think of it without remembering Newman's striking poem on Jonah. We know that his great refreshment to mind and body was found in music, yet he says—

> 'Our choicest bliss, the green repose
> Of the sweet garden shade';

and that, too in the poem which commences with the beautiful yet almost stern stanzas with which I may well close this chapter:—

> 'Deep in his meditative bower,
>   The tranquil seer reclined,
> Numbering the creepers of an hour,
>   The gourds which o'er him twined.
>
> To note each plant, to rear each fruit
>   Which soothes the languid sense;
> He deemed a safe, refined pursuit—
>   His Lord, an indolence.'
>   —*Lyra Apostolica*   *'Jonah.'*

INDEX